New Forest

Compact Guide: New Forest is the ideal quick-reference guide to one of Britain's loveliest national parks. It tells you all you need to know about its attractions, from the villages and walks in the Forest itself to the surrounding cities of Chichester, Salisbury and Portsmouth.

This is just one title in *Apa Publications'* new series of pocket-sized, easy-to-use guidebooks intended for the independent-minded traveller. *Compact Guides* pride themselves on being up-to-date and authoritative. They are in essence mini travel encyclopedias, designed to be comprehensive yet portable, as well as readable and reliable.

Star Attractions

An instant reference to some of the New Forest's most popular tourist attractions to help you on your way.

Longdown Dairy Farm p19

Beaulieu p20

The Needles p25

Bournemouth p27

Kingston Lacy p30

Salisbury Cathedral p33

Winchester p37

Hillier Arboretum p45

Carisbrooke Castle p47

Portchester Castle p52

Southsea fun-fair p57

New Forest

Introduction

Places

Culture

Leisure

Practical Information

The New Forest – Wild at Heart

The New Forest was created in 1079 as a hunting reserve for the king and his courtiers. The penalties for trespassing in the Forest included mutilation, blinding or death. Today the Forest is a playground for the whole of the south of England, receiving 9½ million visitors a year – more, per square mile than any other National Park in Great Britain. New laws – not quite as harsh as those imposed by William the Conqueror – have been introduced to mitigate the erosive effects of so many visitors, but the Forest remains, in essence, a wilderness – especially if you visit out of season, or penetrate those parts that the car cannot reach.

Cherished wilderness

Much of the environmental pressure comes from the fact the Forest is encircled by some of the most densely built-up cities and suburbs in England. From Gosport to Southampton in the east, and from Lymington all along the coast and up to Ringwood in the west, there is scarcely any open country to mark the boundary between one settlement and the next.

Free rein

5

This makes the Forest – the undeveloped hole in the middle – all the more precious. As John R. Wise wrote prophetically more than 100 years ago: 'The New Forest is as much a necessity to the country as the parks are now to London. Land has higher and nobler offices to perform than to support houses or grow corn: to nourish not so much the body as the mind of man; to gladden the eye with its loveliness' (*The New Forest, its History and Scenery*, 1863).

Location and size

The New Forest occupies a roughly square-shaped area of land, 150 square miles (388 sq km) in extent, at the mid-point of England's southern coast. The Solent forms the southern boundary, a stretch of water that separates the Isle of Wight from the mainland, and one of the busiest shipping lanes in England, lively with every size of craft, from leisure dinghies to sleek yachts, container ships, tankers, cross-Channel ferries, submarines and battleships, all heading for the port towns of Portsmouth, Gosport and Southampton.

These densely built-up towns form a continuous conurbation, linked by the M27 motorway, along Southampton Water and the River Test, which together form the eastern boundary of the Forest. To the west, the Forest is bounded by the attractive and marshy valley of the River Avon, while to the north the flat sandy heathland of the Forest runs out where it meets the chalk foothills of Cranborne Chase and Salisbury Plain.

Horse power

On the open road

Nobody is left in any doubt about whether they are in or out of the Forest. Cattle grids at all entry points serve to keep cattle, sheep, deer and ponies within the confines of the Forest, where they are otherwise at liberty to wander at will. Large signs, bearing the Forest logo, carry a welcoming message and a warning about speeding in the Forest: the mandatory 40 mph (64kph) speed limit is designed to prevent collisions between motorists and wandering ponies.

Forest Rule

Such speed limits form part of the panoply of measures introduced in recent years to try and tip the balance back in favour of nature and halt the progressive erosion of a the forest way of life. Several different bodies are involved in the management of the Forest, and it has not always been easy to achieve a consensus. All agree, however, that the landscape is at risk from tourist pressures, hence recent bylaws to restrict camping to designated areas. Mountain bikers, too, must stick to purpose-made tracks. There is talk of banning dogs, restricting horse-riding and imposing punitive parking charges on visitors.

Two key bodies are involved in the running of the Forest, namely the Crown and the Verdurers. Their rights and responsibilities date back to the 11th century when William the Conqueror first designated the New Forest (known in the legal documents of the time by the Latin name of Nova Foresta) as a royal hunting reserve. As such it was subject to Forest Law, designed to keep commoners out and to punish anyone who interfered with the wildlife – such as the red and fallow deer, the wild boar and the wolves – that the king so loved to hunt.

Commoners could not be excluded totally, however. Some actually lived in the Forest and enjoyed property rights. The king's subjects – or rather their pigs – were also rather useful in the autumn because they foraged for oak mast (the raw green acorns of the oak tree) which were poisonous to deer. In time, a compromise evolved whereby the Foresters were given certain rights to compensate them for the restrictions imposed by Forest Law. They could not, for example, enclose land, grow crops or do anything that would restrict the open space available to browsing deer. They could, however, turn out their ponies, donkeys, cattle, pigs or sheep at certain times of year, treating the forest as one large grazing pasture, and they were allowed to dig turf for fuel and take the branchwood of fallen trees.

These and other rights were – and still are - administered by the Verderers, a body of 10 men and women, five of whom are elected by Forest residents, while the other five are appointed to represent official bodies, such

Farming thrives

as the Forestry Commission and the New Forest District Council. The Verderers hold an open court every two months at the Verderers' Hall, in Lyndhurst, and any member of the public has the right to request that they investigate an issue to do with Forest management. The Verderers court – considered to be the oldest court of law in England – is a relic of Norman legal practice, but it serves the Forest well.

From the visitor's point of view, the Verderers' work is visible in the provision of car parks, cattle grids, camping sites, fences and information boards. They pay for these amenities work by levying a small charge on the animals owned by the Commoners, whose free-grazing ponies are such an endearing feature of the New Forest.

Female Forester

The Forest Economy

Just as the Verderers' Court is medieval in origin, so is the Forest economy. The two most important commodities are timber and ponies. Though the ponies appear to be wild, they do, in fact, all belong to one of the 350 Commoners who enjoy grazing rights by virtue of owning land or property within the Forest. There are around 3,000 ponies loose in the Forest at any one time, and each pony is branded by its owner. Five Agisters (pronounced 'ajisters') are employed by the Verderers to oversee the general welfare of the ponies in the wild and tend to any that fall sick or become injured. Each agister patrols a different area of the New Forest. Their work is also paid for by a levy on each animal.

Free to forage

Every autumn the Commoners organise a series of round-ups, called drifts, when the ponies are impounded for marking and for a general health check. Agisters clip the tails of the ponies according to a unique pattern as a sign that the grazing levy has been paid. At this stage, some ponies may also be selected for sale. Sales take place at Beaulieu Road, in the market right next to the railway station, and are a very popular event. Some of the ponies are bought for riding, though many are also sold for meat to the Continent.

Forest legend has it that the first New Forest ponies swam ashore from a wrecked Spanish galleon, though their true origins remain obscure. The Victorians tried to improve the stock in the hope of breeding larger ponies for use as beasts of burden, but the newly bred were not hardy enough to survive the harsh Forest winter and sparse grazing, and most of the ponies have now reverted to the hardier wild type.

Commoners cannot make a living from the sale of ponies alone, and most have full-time jobs, some of them working for the Forestry Commission, which is the other partner, with the Verderers, in the management of the For-

7

est. Around 35 percent of the Forest is unenclosed grazing land. The remainder consists of Crown land managed by the Forestry Commission for timber production; much of this is enclosed to prevent damage from grazing deer. Timber grown in the Forest is used locally for building, fencing, telegraph poles, fuel and garden furniture, while some is exported for use in paper production and chipboard manufacture.

The evolution of the Forest from a royal hunting ground to timber resource has happened slowly over many centuries. In order to create the New Forest, William the Conqueror had oak, beech and other hardwoods planted to improve the gorse-covered heath. Some 200 years later, these trees were of just the right size and maturity to make good shipbuilding material, and so the felling began.

Natural resources

The New Forest has always been a convenient source of timber, because of its proximity to the naval ship-building yards at Bucklers Hard, Southampton, Portsmouth and Gosport. The Napoleonic Wars almost denuded the Forest of all its mature deciduous trees. Fortunately in 1808 the Crown embarked on a 60-year replanting programme, the fruits of which are now visible in the statuesque trees that line the main Forest thoroughfares.

Forest wildlife

Just one of a variety of habitats

Sensitive management of the Forest as a timber resource has led to a variety of different habitats, from open deciduous woodland, where deer roam and mushroom connoisseurs hunt for trophies in the autumn, to wetland, bogs and heath. The Forestry Commission, once wedded to factory-scale production based on fast-growing and densely planted coniferous trees, has recently adopted a more enlightened approach. Mixed woodland is now the norm, with coniferous trees being taken out as thinnings after 20 or 30 years, leaving the deciduous oaks, sweet chestnut and beech trees to grow on to maturity.

Born free

Mammals and reptiles within the Forest are elusive, and the best place to see them is not in the wild, but at the excellent New Forest Nature Quest (*see page 19*), where you can see captive stoats, foxes, field mice and other animals kept in an environment very close to their natural habitat. Insects, plant-life and birds are more easily tracked down in the wild, and information boards throughout the Forest will tell you what to look for.

Some forms of wildlife are regarded as a pest. Grey squirrels, introduced in the 1940s from America, have driven out the native red squirrels, which now only survive as a small colony on Brownsea Island and the Isle of Wight (*see page 28*). Squirrels do great damage by stripping the bark from seedlings and mature trees. Foxes feed on the squirrels, but do not take sufficient numbers to keep the population in balance. Deer are a problem, too, because of their grazing habits, but they can be restricted to certain areas of the Forest by fencing. Herds of deer can sometimes by glimpsed through the woodland, and carrying binoculars is a good idea if you want to take a close look at them.

The undrained Forest is full of bogs, marshes, flooded pits, streams and ponds, all of which make a wonderful wetland habitat for some of Britain's rarest species. As well as frogs, toads and common newts, you may be fortunate to see the protected great crested newt. Carnivorous plants, such as sundews, feed on the local damselflies, while dragonflies buzz noisily through the air at speeds of up to 18mph (30kph) in search of flies and other insect prey. Even butterflies are not immune from the predatory eye of the dragonfly, and the air in the Forest in summer can be unbelievably crowded with nectar-seeking gatekeepers, meadow browns, skippers and ringlets, joined by rarer silver-washed fritillaries, commas, coppers, blues and hairstreaks.

Open heathland forms the largest single habitat type in the Forest. During the summer months, with the bell heather and ling in bloom, this is a bird-lover's paradise, the air full of the varied cries and songs of skylarks, woodlarks, meadow pipits, the cuckoo and the tiny Dartford warbler. After dark, you may even be fortunate enough to hear the unmistakeable 'churr' of the nightjar, a rare and secretive bird that nests on the open heath but is so well camouflaged as to be invisible.

If you are out at night, the sky in the Forest is another source of awe. Parts of the Forest are still far enough away from any town to be truly dark, and the sight of the Milky Way streaming overhead is one good reason for taking a stroll after dark.

Forest friend or foe?

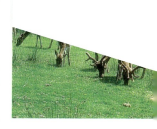

9

Deep in the Forest

Historical Highlights

6500BC Nomadic hunter-gatherer peoples exploit the wooded New Forest for fish and game. A settlement is established at Hengistbury Head, where archaeologists have found arrow heads, flint scrapers for dresssing animal skins, and flint knives for working bone and antler.

1,800BC The lack of prehistoric settlement in the Forest suggests that it is densely wooded until the Bronze Age. Burial mounds in the Forest point to the beginning of woodland clearance.

1,000BC Hengistbury Head develops into a major Iron Age settlement and industrial site, where local iron ore is smelted, coins are minted and Kimmeridge Shale is turned into jewellery.

600BC Construction of the massive ramparts around the Iron Age hillfort at Badbury Rings.

500BC The Iron-Age hillfort constructed at Old Sarum, outside Salisbury.

450BC St Catherine's Hill, outside Winchester, settled as an Iron-Age trading centre.

AD43 After the Roman invasion, new cities are established, including Southampton (Roman Clausentium) and Winchester (Venta Belgarum).

250 The New Forest has a thriving pottery industry, producing the fine reddish-black beakers and jugs seen in Winchester's City Museum.

285–93 Porchester Castle is built during the reign of the Emperor Carausius.

648 Winchester's first Christian church is founded.

690 Founding of Hamwic, the Saxon predecessor of modern Southampton.

829 Egbert makes Winchester the capital of England.

871 King Alfred makes Winchester the main centre of learning in his kingdom.

1066 William the Conqueror is crowned at Winchester.

1079 William the Conqueror declares the New Forest to be a protected royal hunting reserve. Construction of Winchester Cathedral begins.

1086 The Domesday Book is compiled in Winchester.

1100 William (Rufus) II is killed while hunting in the Forest. He is buried beneath Winchester cathedral tower, a fact blamed for its collapse seven years later.

1137 Henry de Blois founds the Hospital of St Cross at Winchester, the first institution of its type in England.

1150 Founding of the priories at Christchurch and Romsey.

1160 The illuminated Winchester Bible, one of the finest artworks of the Middle Ages, is created.

1204 Beaulieu Abbey is founded, the only church institution to be created by King John.

1207 Henry III is born at Winchester Castle.

1220–58 Construction of Salisbury cathedral.

1250–80 The datespan given to Winchester's Round Table by tree-ring analysis.

1280–1310 The addition of Salisbury cathedral's spire.

1382 William of Wykeham founds Winchester College.

1386 Salisbury cathedral's clock is installed, now the oldest working clock in the world.

1483 The New Forest Act allows areas of the New Forest to be enclosed for the first time in order to protect timber stocks from being damaged by grazing deer.

1509–11 Construction of the *Mary Rose* at Portsmouth Dockyard.

1520 Henry VIII entertains the Holy Roman Emperor, Charles V, in Winchester Castle.

1535–40 The Dissolution of the English and Welsh monasteries results in the great estates of Beaulieu, Romsey, Mottisfont, Christchurch and Titchfield being sold off or given to friends of Henry VIII, and the destruction of the shrine of St Swithun in Winchester cathedral.

1540s Henry VIII orders the construction of fortifications to guard the entrance to the Solent, using masonry from Beaulieu Abbey, resulting in the Hurst and Calshot castles in the Forest and Weymouth Castle on the Isle of Wight.

1545 The *Mary Rose* sinks in Portsmouth's harbour.

1554 Mary Tudor marries Philip of Spain in Winchester Cathedral.

1603 Sir Walter Raleigh is found guilty of treason in Winchester Castle's Great Hall.

1611 Felling of New Forest timber specifically to meet the shipbuilding needs of the Royal Navy.

1647 Charles I is incarcerated at Carisbrooke Castle (the Isle of Wight) and Hurst Castle (New Forest) before his trial and execution in London.

1662 Charles II marries Catherine of Braganza in Portsmouth's Garrison Church.

1683 Izaak Walton, author of *The Compleat Angler*, is buried in Winchester cathedral.

1696 The first ship is built at Bucklers Hard.

1698 Peter the Great of Russia visits Portsmouth Dockyard to study shipbuilding.

1765 The launch of *HMS Victory*.

1776 Scots pine is introduced to the Forest, beginning a process that will change the character of the woodland from deciduous to coniferous.

1805 Nelson is killed on board *HMS Victory* during the Battle of Trafalgar.

1808 Beginning of a large-scale replanting programme to replace the woodland of the Forest.

1812 Charles Dickens is born in Portsmouth.

1817 Jane Austen dies in Winchester.

1845 Prince Albert designs Osborne House, Queen Victoria's retreat on the Isle of Wight.

1847 Shipbuilding ceases at Bucklers Hard, as the age of timber gives way to the age of iron.

1851 Deer Removal Act fails in its intention, which is to destroy all the deer remaining in the Forest to protect newly planted trees.

1850s and '60s The last castles to be built in England are constructed at Fort Brockhurst and Fort Nelson to defend Portsmouth Harbour.

1860 Launch of *HMS Warrior*, the world's first iron-clad ship (now in Portsmouth Dockyard).

1901 Queen Victoria dies on the Isle of Wight.

1912 *The Titanic* sets sail from Southampton and sinks on her maiden voyage.

1924 The Forestry Commission takes over management of the New Forest.

1939–45 The New Forest is used for training troops. Southampton, Portsmouth and Gosport suffer heavily from German bombing raids.

1944 Portsmouth and Gosport play a central role in the D-Day allied landings in Normandy.

1949 The New Forest Act, confirming the rights of Verderers and Commoners.

1982 *Mary Rose* rises from beneath the sea and is put on public display.

1987 and 1990 Large numbers of mature New Forest trees are lost in winter gales.

1992 Government proposes to give Heritage Area status to the New Forest.

1994 Protests against M3 link through Twyford Down on the outskirts of Winchester.

1996 The administrative status of the New Forest remains undefined pending a review of the future of the Forestry Commision and of local authority responsibilities.

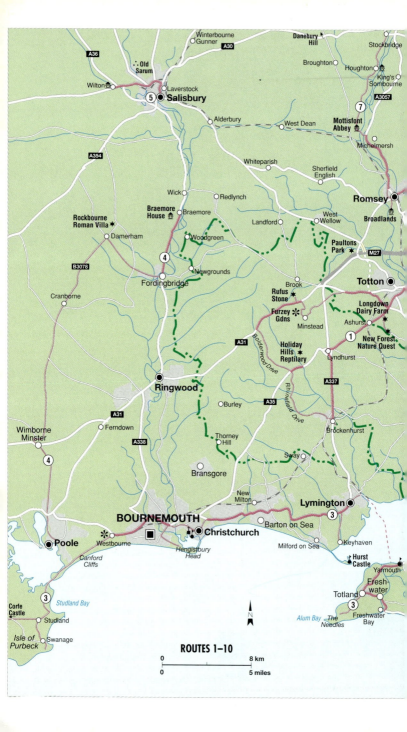

ROUTES 1–10

| 0 | | | | 8 km |
| 0 | | | 5 miles | |

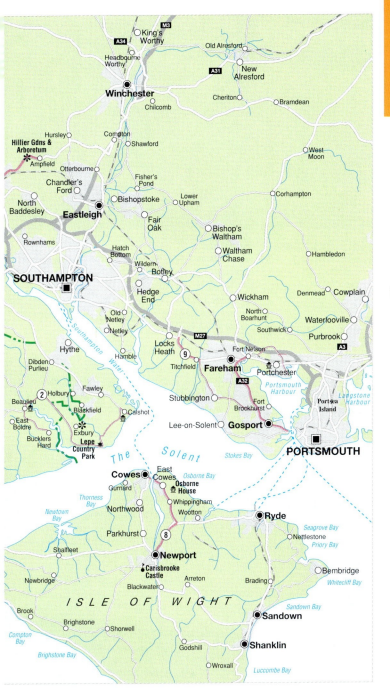

Lyndhurst
Previous pages: Corfe Castle

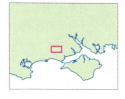

Route 1

Forest Foray

**Lyndhurst – Brockenhurst – Ober Water – Rhine-
field – Bolderwood – Paultons Park – Minstead –
Ashurst – Lyndhurst**

This route provides an introduction to the attractions of
the Forest and takes the form of a circular tour, 26 miles
(42km) in length. Along the route are walks for those who
want to explore the Forest's deeper secrets, plus indoor attractions and theme parks for those inevitable rainy days.

Lyndhurst styles itself as the 'capital' of the New Forest on the strength that this is where the Verderers, who
manage the Forest, meet and hold court. Verderers' Hall
is not open to the public, but you can learn all about it at
the excellent ★★ **New Forest Museum & Visitor Centre** (High Street, Lyndhurst, Hants SO43 7NY; tel: 01703
283914; open 10am–5pm, with later opening in summer).
The tour begins with a short slide programme, which is
a rather uninformative puff for the Forestry Commission,
but the rest of the displays are more meaty, packing in a
huge amount of information on the history, culture and
wildlife of the Forest. Quiz sheets are available for children, and the sounds of ducks, geese and hens that follow you around the centre come from a re-creation of a
typical Forest smallholding at the turn of the century. The
Visitor Information Centre is next door to the museum,
so you can pick up maps and leaflets while here (tel: 01703
282269; same address and opening hours as museum).

One of the well-known personalities featured in the museum is Alice Liddell, the girl for whom Lewis Carroll

First port of call

wrote the *Alice in Wonderland* and *Alice Through the Looking Glass* stories. Later in life Alice moved to Lyndhurst to become Mrs Reginald Hargreaves, and it is under that name that you will find her buried in a rather plain tomb in Lyndhurst churchyard, on the south side of the ★ **church**. The church itself is an exuberant building of red brick built in 1858–70, full of outstanding stained glass by William Morris and Burne-Jones, with lifesize figures of angels supporting the timber roof and a frescoed reredos by Lord Leighton (1864).

Alice Liddell's grave

Another church of great interest is to be found at **Brockenhurst**, 4 miles (6km) south of Lyndhurst along the A337. The ★ **church** is not in the village centre, but signposted off to the left (east) after the level crossing and railway station. Founded in AD800, the church was rebuilt many times and is a patchwork of medieval and later building – the north aisle, unusually, has iron columns, rather than stone. The real interest lies in the churchyard where the massive Brockenhurst yew is said to be over 1,000 years old and one of England's oldest trees.

Nearby is a fascinating headstone marking the grave of Henry 'Brusher' Mills (1840–1905), a Forest character who gained his nickname while working as a groundsman, responsible for brushing cricket pitches to keep them level. Later in life he chose the more unusual profession of snake catcher (the headstone is carved with a portrait of the bearded Mills holding a handful of snakes like some Old Testament prophet). Mills sold the adders he caught to various zoos, while others got turned into 'adder fat' which he sold for medicinal purposes.

Brockenhurst church

Brockenhurst village on the western side of the A337 is a good place to stock up with picnic provisions. At the western end of the High Street is a shallow ford; turning right beyond the ford (signposted Rhinefield) will take you to three of the Forest's finest beauty spots. The first is ★ **Ober Water**, signposted on the right after 1 mile (1.6km). Ober Water is a typical Forest stream, alive with minnows and the occasional brown trout, where the boggy margins support such wildflowers as the bog asphodel, with its beautiful yellow flowers, and the insect-eating sundew plant. Information boards at the car park indicate a choice of walks along the stream lasting up to an hour. If you are lucky, you may catch sight of a kingfisher.

About a mile (2km) further along the same road you will reach ★ **Rhinefield Drive**. This was once a private road leading to Rhinefield House, and, as such, it was planted with a wealth of ornamental trees and shrubs in the mid-19th century. Giant conifers, some over 150 ft (46m) high, form the upper storey, but it is the colourful rhododendrons and azaleas that really pull the crowds

Rhinefield Drive

when they are in full bloom from late April through to early June. Again, there is a choice of walks around this arboretum, which also takes in Blackwater river, so called because of the peaty colour of the water.

A short way north of the Rhinefield Drive car parks, the road meets the A35. Turn right here if you want to visit the ★ **Holidays Hill Reptilary**, found a short distance up on the left, where the Forestry Commission has constructed a series of tanks to display such elusive creatures as smooth snakes, sand lizards and great crested newts.

Returning to the point where you joined the A35, turn right (north) to join the ★ **Bolderwood Drive**, planted in the early 19th century with Douglas fir and western hemlock. About 2 miles (3km) on, you can park at the Bolderwood car park and follow one of the arboretum walks, keeping an eye open for red, fallow and roe deer, which may be spotted grazing in the distance (to the north of the arboretum is a deer observation platform). Continuing north, you pass the memorial to Canadian servicemen who were stationed in the New Forest awaiting deployment in the D-Day landings of 1944.

Another death is commemorated by the ★ **Rufus Stone**, at Upper Canterton, 2 miles (3km) east, and just to the north of the A31. Though called a stone, the monument erected by the Earl de la Warr in 1865 is in fact made of cast iron. It stands on the site of an older stone memorial to King William II, better know as Rufus for his fiery red hair and beard, who was shot while hunting in the Forest in August 1100. There is no evidence whatsoever that this was the spot on which the king was killed, but it is as good a spot as any to erect a monument.

From this part of the Forest, several attractions are within easy reach. If you have children who want to let off steam, try ★★ **Paultons Park** (just north of junction 2 on the M27; tel: 01703 814455; open mid-March to October daily from 10am), the New Forest's answer to Disneyland. The landscaped gardens of the leisure park include ponds, aviaries, Dinosaur Land, the Rio Grande railway, bumper boats and go-karts, a Romany Museum exhibiting beautifully decorated horse-drawn caravans, adventure playgrounds and pirate ships, crazy golf and more.

Quieter pleasures are to be enjoyed at **Minstead**, the picture-postcard village of thatched houses just south of the A31. One such 16th-century cottage, now open to the public and used to display local crafts, stands at the centre of ★**Furzey Gardens**, an 8-acre (3.2 hectare) garden filled with azaleas, heathers and other acid-loving plants (tel: 01703 812464; open daily, except Christmas Day and Boxing Day, 10am–5pm). ★**Minstead church**, with its three-decker pulpit, looks down on the grave of Sir Arthur

Beside Bolderwood Drive

Canadian memorial
Rufus Stone

At Paultons Park

Conan Doyle (1859–1930). Doyle is, of course, famous for his Sherlock Holmes novels, but one of his less-well-known books, *The White Company* (1891) is set in and around the New Forest. Doyle's tombstone, on the south side of the churchyard, is inscribed 'Steel true, blade straight' and reminds us that he was a doctor, practising in Portsmouth and London, as well as a man of letters.

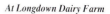

Chocolate-box image

19

From Minstead there is a choice of routes to **Ashurst**, 3 miles (5km) to the east, where two different animal-based attractions compete for custom. The ★ **Longdown Dairy Farm** (Longdown, Ashurst, Hants, SO40 4UH; recorded information tel: 01703 293313; enquiries tel: 01703 293326; open April to October, 10am–5pm) allows children to handle goats and rabbits, feed calves, lambs and piglets, and learn all about milk production (milking time is around 2.30pm).

At Longdown Dairy Farm

A short distance along the same road is the ★★ **New Forest Nature Quest** (same address; tel: 01703 292 408; open daily, except Christmas Day, 10am–5pm). Here British mammals, fish and birds – including deer, foxes, badgers, water voles, hedgehogs, ferrets, stoats, mice, rats and barn owls – are displayed in a series of old farm buildings and forest enclosures that approximate to their natural habitat. Some of the animals are natural exhibitionists and show off for the benefit of visitors. Others are more shy, but miniature cameras within their enclosures, linked to TV monitors, allow a close-up view of their activities, whether building their nests or feeding their young. Knowledgeable staff give short talks throughout the day. The site also includes a reptilary and a butterfly tunnel, displaying British butterflies and moths. Altogether, this is an ideal way to meet the creatures that inhabit the Forest, and you may find yourself spending far longer here than you expected, not to mention developing a sneaking respect for the industry of the average British rat.

Route 2

The Heart of the Forest

Beaulieu – Bucklers Hard – Exbury Gardens – Lepe Country Park – Calshot Castle

For many visitors, Beaulieu is the primary reason for venturing into the New Forest. The stately home, ruined abbey, gardens and National Motor Museum are enough to keep one busy for the best part of a day, but you can also walk down the Beaulieu River to the 18th-century maritime village of Bucklers Hard, or head for the southeastern tip of the Forest and enjoy the views from Calshot Castle.

Calshot Castle

20

★★★ **Beaulieu** (tel: 01590 612345; open daily, Easter to September 10am–6pm, October to Easter 10am–5pm, closed Christmas Day) was one of the first stately homes in England to open its doors to the public. When Lord Montagu inherited the estate on his 25th birthday, in 1951, he set about turning it into one of the country's most popular visitor attractions, best known as the home of the National Motor Museum.

Beaulieu (pronounced 'Bewlee' and derived from the Latin *bellus locus*, or 'beautiful place') has long been an integral part of the Forest. King John, not especially known for his piety, dreamt that he was in hell being whipped by monks in white habits. Taking this as a warning, he decided to placate the fury of God by donating a tract of land to the Cistercian order, who wore white habits as a symbol of purity, as distinct from the black and brown habits of the Benedictines and Franciscans.

The first monks arrived in 1204, and they built the magnificent **abbey** that now only survives as a roofless ruin.

Lord Montagu of Beaulieu

This stands alongside the Palace House, beyond the very ugly building that houses the Motor Museum, and is the best place to begin a tour of Beaulieu's attractions.

The surviving walls and columns hint at the size and grandeur of the abbey complex, which had the largest Cistercian abbey church in England, 336 ft (102m) in length and 182ft (55m) wide. The cloister, to the south of the church, is the best preserved part of the abbey and is now planted with herbs. It is just possible to imagine the monks sunning themselves here during the few hours of the day when they were allowed to relax from a monotonous routine of prayers, study and services.

Abbey Cloister and church

On the south side of the cloister is the monks' refectory, or dining room, now converted to form the **parish church** for Beaulieu village. The church retains its hall-like character, and the magnificent pulpit, on the right hand-side, is where the Bible would have been read to the monks as they ate their simple meals of oatmeal gruel, bread, beans, eggs, vegetables or fish.

The wealth of the abbey depended on the hard work of lay brothers who did not take monastic vows but lived a strict regime and managed the farms attached to the abbey. The Domus building, home to the lay brothers, has survived in its entirety to the west of the cloister and this now houses displays on monastic life at Beaulieu.

21

Along with all the other monasteries in England, Beaulieu was confiscated by Henry VIII in the 1530s, at the Dissolution, and the monks were pensioned off. Parts of the abbey were demolished and the stone reused to construct Calshot Castle (the last place to be visited in this tour). Henry then sold the abbey and its 8,000-acre (3,200-hectare) estate to the Earl of Southampton. The estate produced a handsome income, and the habitable parts of the abbey were used as a hunting lodge, but it was not until 1867 that the estate had its first resident owner, Lord Henry Scott, grandfather of the present Lord Montagu.

Scott turned the abbey gatehouse into the large baronial-style **Palace House** that stands next to the abbey ruins. Wandering through the house, it is possible to see how the central archway of that medieval gatehouse has been filled in to accommodate the massive and ornately carved fireplaces that warm the house. The beautifully vaulted ceilings survive, and the walls are hung with portraits of Lord Montagu's ancestors and present family. Actors playing the part of butler and housemaid will let you into some of the more intimate secrets of the house (and for a small extra payment, you can ask the butler if you can see the private apartments used by the present occupants, providing that his Lordship is not at home).

Maid service

From the Palace House you can walk through the attractive gardens to the **National Motor Museum**, hop

At the Motor Museum

on a vintage open-topped bus that drives a circular route through the grounds or queue for a ride on the monorail that encircles the grounds at a height of 30ft (9m), giving a fine aerial view of the gardens.

The National Motor Museum began as a collection of five historic vehicles inherited by Lord Montagu from his father. Today it has grown into a huge collection covering 100 years of the motor car. It treads very lightly over technical matters, concentrating more on the social history of the car than on torque ratios and cylinder capacities. Apart from the vehicles themselves, displayed in chronological order, there are advertisements and posters to admire, including the famous Shell Collection extolling the delights of the open road. There are also novelty vehicles, trams, buses and fire engines to climb upon and a section devoted to more recent cars – Ford Cortinas, Austin Sevens and Volkswagen Beetles – that will induce nostalgic memories in anyone aged over 40.

Another fascinating display area is centred on cars that have broken the landspeed record, including Golden Arrow and Bluebird. Videos show heroic drivers, such as Sir Malcolm Campbell, speeding across the salt flats of Utah or Lake Eyre, as the record progressively climbs from 39mph/62.8 kph (in 1898) to the present official record of 633.468 mph/1,019.5 kph (unofficially speeds of 739 mph/1,189.3 kph have been achieved). In the Wheels section of the museum your own sedate miniature car takes you around a series of miniature tableaux, complete with smells and appropriate sounds, covering the invention of the first cars, the dawn of mass production, and the likely shape of cars to come.

If all this emphasis on motoring fills you with a desire to escape and walk, then head for the village of **Beaulieu**, park the car and head down the main street to the mill and bridge that carries traffic across the Beaulieu River. Before the bridge, on the right, a public footpath sign takes you to a well-trodden track that crosses fields and passes through mixed woodland, following the river downstream to Bucklers Hard. The walk is well signposted and is just over 5 miles (9km) in distance, so it may be as well to send one of your party in the car to meet you at the other end, otherwise it is a long walk back.

Whether you walk or drive, ★★★ **Bucklers Hard** (tel: 01590 616203; open daily, 10am–6pm March to Spring Bank Holiday, 10am–9pm Spring Bank Holiday to September, 10am–4.30pm rest of year, closed Christmas Day) is a place well worth visiting for its timeless air (and its waterside pub called the Master Builder's House). Visitors to the village any time between 1696 and 1847 would have found the view down the main street blocked by the

Cottages in Bucklers Hard

huge wooden hulls of merchant and naval ships under construction in the slipways at the river's edge. The shipyard was sited here because of the ready availability of timber from the New Forest and the depth of the river at this point, which was sufficient to allow for the launch and passage of huge state-of-the-art warships.

Just about everyone who lived in the one-street village worked in shipbuilding, whether as carpenters, sawyers, blacksmiths, rope and sailmakers or labourers. Their lives are brought to life through a series of models and reconstructed cottage interiors in the **Maritime Museum** at the head of the main street. In the street itself, you can visit a home of a shipwright, furnished as it would have been when it was the home of Thomas Burlace and his family between 1781 and 1816.

At the Maritime Museum

As you stand on the bank of the Beaulieu River at Bucklers Hard, looking across the forest of masts that fills the nearby yachting marina, you may catch a glimpse of the statuesque trees and colourful azaleas of ★★ **Exbury Gardens**, on the opposite bank. Reaching the garden involves driving back to Beaulieu and crossing the bridge to return down the river's eastern side. The woodland gardens at Exbury (recorded information, tel: 01703 899422; general enquiries, tel: 01703 891203; open daily 10am–5.30pm or dusk, if earlier) were planted in the 1920s by Lionel de Rothschild with rhododendrons, azaleas and camellias as the foundation of the display. More recently, the garden has been enhanced by the addition of ponds and wetland areas, bamboo groves, a rock garden and a rose garden, so that the season of interest spreads from the earliest spring bulbs to the dying embers of the magnificent beech trees in autumn. There is also a plant centre.

23

Azaleas in bloom

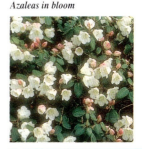

Just south of Exbury, ★ **Lepe Country Park** has a mile of sand and shingle beach with fine views across to the Isle of Wight. Even more extensive views are to be had from ★ **Calshot Castle**, not easily found because it sits in the middle of an active naval base, but well-signposted (B3053 Fawley road). The castle (English Heritage, tel: 01703 892023; open 1 April to 31 October, daily 10am – 6pm, or dusk if earlier) is a relic of Henry VIII's paranoia, being one of a chain of circular fortresses that he built at strategic points along the south coast in the belief that the forces of Catholic Europe would unite and invade England in retaliation for the Reformation and the Dissolution of the Monasteries. The castle was built from stone reused from Beaulieu Abbey and it sits at the tip of a spit jutting into the Solent. Its rooftop observation point commands views that stretch up river towards Southampton (ignoring the bulk of Fawley power station) and south to Cowes on the Isle of Wight.

Calshot Castle

Route 3

The South Coast

Lymington (and the Isle of Wight ferry) – Christchurch – Hengistbury Head – Bournemouth – Studland Bay and Brownsea Island.

Some of England's finest beaches and seaside attractions are to be found along the coastal strip from Lymington to Poole, so pack your swimming costumes and head for the sands, or spend a day exploring the western tip of the Isle of Wight by taking a ferry from Lymington (other parts of the Isle of Wight are covered on pages 46 and 57).

Lymington is a town of considerable size and charm, whose long High Street is lined by dignified Georgian houses. The galleried church is worth a visit, as is the ★ **Museum and Visitor Centre** in New Street, which displays Iron-Age finds from the Buckland Rings fort, located on the north side of the town, and tells the story of the local salt industry.

From the eastern end of the High Street, cobbled lanes, lined with bow-windowed cottages, run down to Fishermans Quay, on the Lymington River, once the haunt of smugglers, now a marina filled with sleek yachts. On the opposite bank is the Wightlink ferry pier, popular with day visitors to the **Isle of Wight** because it takes a mere half-an-hour to cross the Solent from here. The car and passenger ferry departs from the quay at hourly intervals every day from around 6am–9.30pm (if you plan to take your car, be sure to book well in advance; enquiries and reservations, tel: 01705 827744).

The ferry lands at **Yarmouth**, a characterful harbour town at the western end of the island (tourist information centre on The Quay; tel: 01983 760015). The **church** contains a fine statue of Sir Robert Holmes, appointed governor of the Isle of Wight by Charles II in order to bring the strongly Cromwellian island back to heel. The head and the body of the statue are a far from perfect match; Sir Robert captured a French ship in the English Channel and found a statue of Louis XIV on board which he appropriated for his own memorial, removing the French king's head and adding his own.

Cromwell's troops were garrisoned in ★ **Yarmouth Castle**, which stands alongside the ferry terminal (English Heritage; tel: 01983 760678; open 1 April to 31 October, daily, 10am–1pm and 2–6pm or dusk if earlier). This castle was built in 1547 by Henry VIII to defend the western entrance to the Solent, and it forms part of a chain of coastal fortresses along with Hurst Castle and Calshot.

*Lymington
Fisherman's Quay*

Yarmouth Castle

Several tour operators offer boat trips from Yarmouth to the ★ **Needles** (alternatively, you can catch a number 7A or 42 bus), a group of three chalk stacks that have been eroded away from the narrow western tip of the island. Buses also call at **Alum Bay**, famous for the coloured sands to be found in its soft and crumbling cliffs. These may look disappointingly monochrome unless you happen to visit on a rainy day, and you may be pleased or shocked, depending on your point of view, to find that this once wild part of the coast has been turned into a theme park, with dare-devil rides and crazy golf (The Needles Pleasure Park; tel: 01983 752401; open 1 April to 31 October, 10am–5pm, to 6pm in August).

The Needles

A good way to escape the crowds is to follow the **Freshwater Way** footpath from Yarmouth to the ★ **Freshwater**, just under 2 miles (3km) south. This an undemanding walk since the footpath follows the line of an old railway. The church here is associated with the poet laureate Alfred, Lord Tennyson, who lived in Freshwater (at Farringford House, now the Farringford Hotel) between 1853 and his death in 1892. There are memorials to several members of his family, and the stained-glass window by G F Watts portrays Lady Tennyson as an angel. The Freshwater Way continues south to **Freshwater Bay**, where it links up with the Tennyson Trail, a bracing cliff-top walk along the southwestern tip of the island.

25

Back on the mainland, castle fanatics will not want to miss ★ **Hurst Castle**, which is best reached by ferry from Keyhaven, 4 miles (6km) southwest of Lymington (Hurst Castle Ferry; tel: 01425 610784; the same company offers foot passenger ferry services to Yarmouth on the Isle of Wight during the summer months). This is the most sophisticated of the castles built by Henry VIII to defend the Solent, and

Hurst Castle Ferry
Alum Bay

it was here that Charles I was briefly incarcerated before being taken to London for trial and execution.

The ★ **castle** at **Christchurch**, 8 miles (13km) further west, is considerably more accessible, standing as it does in the middle of the town, next to the magnificent Norman ★★★ **priory**. Priory and castle date from the 12th century, and while the simple Norman motte and bailey is now a ruin, the priory remains much as it was when built for the Augustinian monks who arrived here in 1150. As large and dignified as a cathedral, the priory has a full set of medieval misericords, carved with animals, clowns and acrobats, and a huge stone reredos carved with a Tree of Jesse, tracing the lineage of Christ. The central scene is a charming depiction of the Nativity. The screen dates from 1350, and is extremely rare, since much stone carving of this kind was destroyed by iconoclastic zealots during the Cromwellian era.

The path that runs northwestwards from the priory leads to the ★★ **Red House**, built in 1764 as the parish workhouse, then converted to a private home and now a fine local history museum (Quay Road, Christchurch, Dorset BH23 1BU; tel: 01202 482860; open Tuesday to Saturday 10am–5pm and Sunday 2–5pm). Apart from good displays of costumes and 1930s furnishings, there is a comprehensive account of the wildlife and the archaeology of Hengistbury Head, one of the most important prehistoric sites in Europe.

Hengistbury Head

Arming yourself with one of the guides to ★★ **Hengistbury Head** sold at the museum, you can visit this clifftop headland by driving to Southbourne, then turning east and following the road until it runs out. From the car park a trail runs round the promontory, with marker posts indicating points of interest, which range from spectacular coastal views to rare chalkland plants and lagoons where oystercatchers search for food.

Various earthworks represent the remains of a major Iron Age settlement which thrived during the first millennium BC. The prosperity of the settlement was based on smelting the ironstone boulders that are found on the seashore. Apart from iron production, the inhabitants specialised in boat building, cloth production, coinage, glass-bead manufacture and lathe-turning to make shale bracelets. Finds from the site indicate that their trade contacts extended to the Mediterranean, and that their diet included imported wine and olive oil.

Looking for buried treasure

From Hengistbury Head westwards to Alum Chine there is now a 7-mile (11-km) stretch of sandy **beach** that offers a huge range of choice, depending on your taste in seaside activity. Most of the seafront is built up with fine Edwardian villas and hotels, so that one resort blends into another. ★ **Southbourne** has a Noddy Train carrying excited children through picturesque woodland to the sandy beach, and ★ **Christchurch** attracts watersports enthusiasts. ★ **Bournemouth** is the biggest of the resorts, and the emphasis here is on family entertainment, with a pier, beach clubs, seafront amusements, miniature train rides and a huge choice of cinemas, shops, discos, theatres and musical entertainment.

If it is the wrong weather for outdoor activities, the Bournemouth area has plenty of indoor attractions as well. Top of the visit list should be the eccentric seaside villa that houses the ★★ **Russell-Cotes Art Gallery and Museum** (East Cliff, Bournemouth; tel: 01202 551009; open Tuesday to Sunday, 10am–5pm). The house, built in 1894, was left to Bournemouth by Sir Merton and Lady Russell-Cotes and is stuffed with exotic Victorian artefacts, objects collected on travels in Africa and the Far East, and titillating paintings of female nudes with titles like *The Bather Alarmed* and *The Dawn of Love*. There are some very fine high Victorian paintings here as well, including Albert Moore's *Midsummer* (1887), and a newly built extension is used to display more modern work and travelling exhibitions.

Bournemouth motifs

Continuing westwards, Canford Cliffs is the location of the ★ **Compton Acres Gardens**, conceived as a museum of different garden styles, from Italian and Japanese to rock, heather and water gardens (tel: 01202 700778; open March to October daily, 10.30am–6.30pm).

★ **Canford Cliffs** and its neighbour, ★ **Branksome**, are linked to the beach by a series of 'chines' – the local name for the deep wooded river valleys that lead down to the sea. Here the atmosphere is more up-market, with fewer amuseument arcades and fast-food restaurants, but nowhere along this popular coast is truly remote during

27

Bournemouth's pier

Head for Studland Beach

Corfe Castle

the main holiday season, and you may have to arrive quite early in the morning to find parking space within comfortable walking distance of a beach.

Beach etiquette tends to be rather staid and British on these beaches, so if you want to take all your clothes off and frolic around in the nude, head for ★ **Studland Beach**, on the **Isle of Purbeck**. One way to reach the beach is on the ferry that links Sandbanks to Shell Bay. Another route is to take one of the ferries from Bournemouth or Poole to Swanage (frequent services daily from 5am–11pm; tel: 01929 450203).

Even if you are not a naturist, the beach here, rated the best in Britain, is worth a visit. Three miles (5km) of clean white sand are backed by the ★ **Studland Heath National Nature Reserve**, a habitat rich in insects, reptiles and wildflowers. The National Trust Visitor Centre alongside the car park at Knoll beach, just north of Swanage, explains the local wildlife.

If you take the car on the ferry, the whole of the Isle of Purbeck is within easy reach for exploration. The main tourist magnet is ★★ **Corfe Castle**, a romantic ruin sitting on a knoll with far reaching views. Built in the 11th century, the castle was stoutly defended by a group of courageous women in 1635, who kept 600 Parliamentary troops at bay and withstood a six-week siege during the Civil War. In revenge, Cromwell had the castle 'slighted' – deliberately wrecked – in 1646.

★ **Swanage** itself was the main port from which Purbeck 'marble', a hard shelly limestone, was shipped to London, where it was used for church building and street paving during the post-Fire rebuilding of the City. Later London gave back one of its finest buildings: the facade of Swanage Town Hall, with its bust of Flora, cherubs and swags, came from the Mercers' Hall in London, which was demolished in 1872 and re-erected here in 1883. North of Swanage is a 2-mile (3-km) clifftop walk to ★ **Old Harry Rocks**, a picturesque spot at the southern end of Studland Beach.

Swanage Town Hall

All aboard for Brownsea Island

From Sandbanks, it is also possible to take a ferry to ★★ **Brownsea Island**, another important wildlife habitat belonging to the National Trust. The 500-acre (200-hectare) expanse of heath and woodland is one of England's last homes to a colony of red squirrels, and it supports such rare species as the silver-studded butterfly, the Dartford warbler and the sand lizard. There is a large heronry, and the shallow waters of the lagoons around the island attract large numbers of seabirds. The best way to discover the wildlife is to join a guided walk (book in advance by contacting the warden, tel: 01202 709445).

Route 4

Ringwood Forest

Poole – Wimborne Minster – Kingston Lacy – Badbury Rings – Cranborne Manor – Rockbourne Roman Villa – Fordingbridge – Breamore House

The A338, running from the south coast up to Salisbury, marks the western boundary of the New Forest, while to the west of the road lies Ringwood Forest and the rolling chalk downlands of Cranborne Chase, another ancient royal hunting reserve. This route, which many travellers drive on their way to and from the New Forest, offers a variety of sites, from the seaside attractions of Poole and the Old Master paintings at Kingston Lacy, to the impressive Iron-Age earthworks at Badbury Rings and the delightful gardens of Cranborne Manor.

★**Poole** is an ancient and still thriving port situated on the rim of one of the largest natural harbours in the world. Ferries depart from here for Brownsea Island (*see page 28*) and for destinations further afield, such as Guernsey, Jersey, Cherbourg and St Malo. The sheltered, almost landlocked harbour is popular for watersports and dinghy sailing, which is one of the reasons why Sir Robert Baden-Powell chose Brownsea Island as a base for the first ever Boy Scouts' adventure camp in 1907.

A whole gallery at the town's ★★ **Waterfront Museum** (Poole Quay; tel: 01202 683138; open Monday to Saturday 10am–5pm, Sunday 2–5pm) is devoted to the story of scouting. The museum is housed in one of the old warehouses lining the waterfront, and its lively displays cover the archaeology and history of Poole, with a reconstruc-

Bright and breezy image

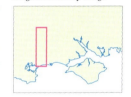

Gone fishing

On the waterfront

Minster church

Kingston Lacy and its sundial

tion of an Iron-Age log boat, a glimpse into the secret world of the smuggler and a look at some of the historic wrecks lying beneath the waters of the harbour. Almost next door is the ★ **Scaplen's Court Museum** (High Street; same telephone number and opening times as Waterfront Museum), set in a medieval merchant's house and telling the story of domestic life in Poole through the ages. There is an excellent craft shop attached to this museum, while a short distance away is the **Poole Pottery**, founded in 1873 and famous for its early arts-and-crafts designs. Visitors can tour the pottery and have a go at making a pot on a wheel (Poole Quay; tel: 01202 666200; open daily 9am–5.30pm, or later in summer).

Leaving Poole on the A349 northwards, it is 6 miles (10km) to **Wimborne Minster**, where the twin towers of the imposing ★★ **Minster church** rise above the rooftops of the town's Georgian houses. Founded in 705 by Cuthburga, sister of King Ina of Wessex, the original minster was destroyed by the Danes and the present church dates from the Norman refounding. The **Chained Library**, off the south aisle, contains rare 13th-century manuscripts and was founded in 1686 not just for the use of the clergy, but also for the people of Wimborne, who proudly claim this to be England's first free public library.

Opposite the minster is the **Priest's House Museum of East Dorset Life** (23 High Street; tel: 01202 882533; open 1 April to 31 October, Monday to Saturday 10.30am–5pm and Sunday 2–5pm). The attractions here include a working Victorian kitchen, an archaeology gallery where you are encouraged to touch the objects, a Georgian parlour and a Victorian stationer's shop, not to mention a fine garden and tea room.

Fridays, Saturdays and Sundays are **market** days in Wimborne, but this is no ordinary small-town market: the huge covered bazaar extends to 5 acres (2 hectares), has its own multi-storey car park and attracts over 300 stallholders, many dealing in antiques and bric-a-brac.

Just west of Wimborne, on the B3082, is the National Trust-owned ★★★ **Kingston Lacy**, a 17th-century house containing works by Rubens, Titian, Van Dyck and Lely (tel: 01202 883402; open 1 April to 31 October, Saturday to Wednesday, park 11.30am–6pm or dusk if earlier, house noon–5.30pm). The mansion is set in the midst of a 250-acre (100-hectare) park which has always been farmed by traditional organic methods. The result is a wonderfully rich ecology, with rare meadow flowers and butterflies in relative abundance. Red Devon cattle graze the park, adding to the sense of rural tranquillity.

Two miles (3km) further along the same road is the Iron-Age hillfort known as ★ **Badbury Rings** because of its concentric series of defensive ditches and banks. Inevitably the site has attracted legends, including one claiming it as the site of King Arthur's last battle with the treacherous Mordred. There are fine views from the summit of the camp and it is a good place to children to let off steam pretending to be Knights of the Round Table – or, to be more archaeologically accurate, pre-Roman Celtic warriors.

Back in Wimborne, the B3078 northwards makes an attractive drive along the edge of Cranborne Chase to the ruined Norman church at ★ **Knowlton**, which stands in the middle of neolithic henge monument (English Heritage, always open). Pretty **Cranborne** has one of England's most appealing gardens, set around the Jacobean ★★ **manor** and originally planted by John Tradescant, sadly only open one day a week (Wednesday, 9am–5pm from March to September; tel: 01725 517248). The garden is wonderfully varied and ranges from the formal avenues and topiary of Tradescant's 17th-century design to the romantic plantings of clematis and roses.

Knowlton church

The B3078 winds northeastwards for 3 miles (5km) to Damerham, where a side road heads for ★ **Rockbourne Roman Villa** (tel: 01725 518541; open April to October, Monday to Friday 2–6pm, July, August and weekends 10.30am–6pm). The luxurious villa, with over 46 rooms, dates from the 2nd century AD and has some fine mosaic floors. A small museum on the site displays finds from recent excavations, including coins, pottery and some remarkably well-preserved leather shoes.

At Rockbourne Roman Villa

By continuing along the B3078 you will come to ★ **Fordingbridge**, whose name says it all. The town stands alongside a fine medieval seven-arch bridge spanning the River Avon. The parish church contains a splendid hammer-beam roof decorated with carved angels. The town is surrounded by water meadows, where owls hunt at dusk and herons wade in the tributaries of the Avon.

The busy A338 follows the Avon valley upstream all the way to Salisbury (*see Route 5, page 32*). Our last port of call is ★★ **Breamore House** (pronounced 'Bremmer'), situated 3 miles (5km) north of Fordingbridge (tel: 01725 512468; open 2–5.30pm on Tuesday, Wednesday and Saturday in April, Tuesday, Wednesday, Thursday and weekends in May to July, daily in August). The large late-Elizabethan house enjoys fine views over the Avon valley and is handsomely furnished, but for many families the main attraction will be the countryside museum and adventure playground. While you are here, do not miss Breamore's fascinating Anglo-Saxon ★ **church** which stands next to the house, surrounded by beautiful parkland. The cruciform church dates from around 1020 and has an enigmatic inscription carved over one of the doors.

'The Boy with the Bat', one of Braemore's many paintings

Route 5

Salisbury

Old Sarum – Salisbury Cathedral and Close – Wilton House

*In Salisbury's Close
Old Sarum*

The best palace to begin a visit to Salisbury is not in the town itself, but on a windswept hill 2 miles (3km) north of the city off the A345. ★★ **Old Sarum** is the name of the hill (English Heritage; tel: 01722 335398; open daily 10am–4pm, to 6pm in April to October) and the extensive ruins are all that remains of Salisbury's predecessor. The ruins are set within the massive ramparts of an Iron-Age hillfort built around 500BC. The Norman founders of Old Sarum built their town inside the ready-made fortification, and the remains of the motte and bailey, royal castle and cathedral have survived, though there is little to see of the town itself, whose wooden buildings decayed long ago.

During the early 13th century, the inhabitants of Old Sarum decided to move to the fertile river valley below, where they founded today's city of Salisbury. The reason for the move was well expressed in a letter written by Peter of Blois, a monk at Old Sarum, in 1198. He described the spot as 'exposed to wind, infertile, without water and depopulated'. A few people lived on at Old Sarum at least until Tudor times, and they continued to elect a Member of Parliament until the Reform Act of 1832, which abolished this and several other so-called 'rotten boroughs' (rotten because the seat could effectively be bought and sold). Today, Old Sarum is a beautiful spot marking the boundary between the chalk downland to the north, and the lush water meadows where the rivers Avon, Nadder and Bourne all meet.

Salisbury was rationally planned with a chequer-board grid of streets, large open spaces for holding markets, and streets devoted to certain trades, perpetu-

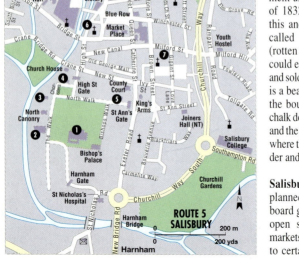

ROUTE 5
SALISBURY

Salisbury Cathedral

33

ated in names like Fish Row, Butcher Row, Silver Street, Poultry Cross and Cheese Market. The huge cathedral was sited at the edge of the town, rather than in the centre, so that it had room to expand. The cathedral community formed a separate miniature township, divided from Salisbury by high walls, enclosing schools, hospitals, theological colleges and clergy housing.

Most people enter the cathedral's **close** through the **High Street Gate**, part of the original close defences designed to separate town from gown. These defences, and several of the oldest houses in the close, were built from masonry reused from the cathedral at Old Sarum, which was deliberately demolished for this purpose. For the new Salisbury cathedral, however, creamy-white limestone was quarried at Chilmark, some 20km (32km) west of Salisbury, and floated on barges down the River Nadder.

The ★★★ **cathedral** ❶ is unique amongst medieval English cathedrals in being built in one campaign, and in one homogeneous style. Started in 1220, it was complete 38 years later, except for the wonderful spire (England's tallest at 123 metres), which was added to the tower as an inspired afterthought between 1280 and 1310. The cathedral, with its statue-carved west front, is a magnificent sight, after which the Early English interior, perhaps because of its very uniformity, can come as a disappointment. The pleasures of the cathedral, however, come from exploring its nooks and crannies, especially the marvellous timber roof (tours of the roof take place regularly and are well worth joining if you have a head for heights).

Nave

Down at ground level, the nave is filled with the tombs of saints, bishops and battle-scarred warriors, such as William Longespée [A] (in the southeast), who died in 1226 and whose tomb is carved with England's oldest armoured effigy, and Sir John Cheney [B] (on the oppo-

Effigy of William Longespée

Interior details

site side of the nave), a giant of a man who served in Henry VIII's bodyguard and who died in 1509. Near Sir John is England's oldest working **clock** [C], installed in 1386 (since when it has ticked more than 500 million times).

Moving eastward, **Bishop Audley's Chantry** [D] in the ambulatory is one of several magnificent 16th-century monuments clustered around the main altar, and the **Lady Chapel** contains the shrine of St Osmund [E] whose bones were moved here from Old Sarum. Off to the south of the nave is the **Cloister**, the largest in England and added in 1263–84 in the Decorated style, which is prettier and more ornate than the Early English of the cathedral. The cloister leads to the **Chapter House**, whose walls are decorated with Old Testament murals. Here is displayed one of the four original copies of Magna Carta, the bill of rights signed by King John in 1215.

Several museums are to be found within the cathedral close. The best of these is the ★★ **Salisbury Museum** ❷ (65 The Close; tel: 01722 332151; open Monday to Saturday 10am–5pm, Sundays in July and August, 2–5pm), housed in the splendid King's House (head over to the left as you exit from the cathedral's west door), so called because James I used to lodge here regularly in the 17th century. The excellent displays here cover such diverse topics as who built Stonehenge and why, to what fashionably dressed citizens of Salisbury wore down the ages.

Turning left from the museum, you will pass the discreetly guarded home of a former Conservative prime minister, before reaching the 15th-century **Wardrobe**, so called because it was originally built as the Bishop of Salisbury's storehouse. It is now home to the ★ **Duke of Edinburgh's Royal Regimental Museum** ❸ (58 The Close; tel: 01722 414536; open April to October, 10am–4.30pm, February, March and November, Monday to Friday 10am–4.30pm, closed December and January) which you may want to visit for a look at the fine timberwork of the medieval hall at the heart of the building.

A short way north of here is ★★ **Mompesson House** ❹,

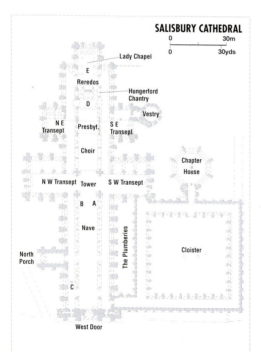

SALISBURY CATHEDRAL

0   30m
0   30yds

Lady Chapel

E

Reredos

Hungerford Chantry

D

Vestry

N E Transept   Presbyt   S E Transept

Choir

Chapter House

N W Transept   Tower   S W Transept

B   A

Nave

The Plumberies

Cloister

North Porch

C

West Door

Malmesbury House

its Queen-Anne facade fronted by wrought-iron railings, where you can pretend to be residents of the close for a while amidst the handsomely furnished 18th-century rooms (National Trust; tel: 01722 335659; open 1 April to 31 October, Saturday to Wednesday, noon–5.30pm). As an interesting experiment, the National Trust has set aside one of the back rooms for visitors to relax, furnished with magazines and comfortable chairs. There is also a walled garden where you can enjoy a light lunch or tea.

If your appetite for historic houses is still not diminished, there is another fine Queen Anne house to see at the northeastern corner of the close, reached by walking along North Walk to the St Ann's Gate. ★★ **Malmesbury House** ❺, (15 The Close; tel: 01722 327027; open at Easter and 2 May to 1 October, Tuesday to Saturday noon–5pm) was built in the 15th-century and considerably enlarged in the 18th century when its rooms, decorated with rococo plasterwork, played host to George Federick Handel.

Exiting the close through the High Street Gate again, a stroll up the High Street will take you to the church of ★★**St Thomas of Canterbury** ❻, with its lovely timber roof (dating from 1450) featuring ornate tracery and angelic musicians. The early 16th-century wall painting shows Christ in Majesty seated on a rainbow and devils seizing the damned.

On the High Street

Leaving the church, turn right and right again to find Minster Street which leads to the ★ **Poultry Cross**. This was built in the 15th century as a covered market, roofed by an ornate stone crown and spirelet. It sits at the centre of a tangle of medieval alleys, such as Butcher Row and Fish Row, lined by timber-framed houses with overhanging upper storeys. Immediately to the north is the ★ **Market Place**, a bustling spot where a fruit and vegetable market takes place most days in front of the rather

Soaking up the sunshine

ugly grey-brick **Guildhall**, built for civic functions in 1788–95. More attractive are the brick and tile-hung houses of **Blue Row** on the north side of the square, many of them Georgian in appearance, but hiding medieval houses behind their facades.

Turning right in Queen Street, on the east side of the square, will take you to Milford Street, where the Red Lion Hotel ❼ has a galleried courtyard where travelling players used to mount their plays. New Canal, leading back to the High Street, was once an open waterway used for transporting goods into the centre from the city's rivers.

In the grounds of Wilton House

Three miles (5km) west of Salisbury, and almost a suburb of the modern city, is the town of **Wilton**, dominated by the ★★★ **Wilton House** estate of the Earl of Pembroke (tel: 01722 743115; open April to October daily, 11am–6pm).

Here you can take your choice from a range of attractions, each with a separate entrance charge. Many people opt just to visit the grounds, with its huge **adventure playground**, one of the best in England, built among the treetops, with rope ladders and walkways.

Wilton House itself is introduced by an excellent 17-minute video on the 450-year-old history of the Pembroke's ownership of the estate. The house, which is built around the remains of an abbey, is an odd-looking building (1636–50) that betrays few of the classical trademarks of its architect, Inigo Jones. Pepys said of Wilton, 'The situation I do not like, nor the house promise much.'

Such would seem to be a fair judgement until you encounter the two glories of the house, the **Cube Room**, measuring $29^1/_2$ft by $29^1/_2$ by $29^1/_2$ (9m by 9 by 9) and the Double Cube Room, measuring 59ft by $29^1/_2$ by $29^1/_2$ (18m by 9 by 9). Both rooms are nobly proportioned and have magnificently frescoed ceilings, while the gilded stucco work of the walls was purpose designed to frame a series of Pembroke family portraits by Van Dyck and his assistants. The rooms look out over the delicate Palladian Bridge (1737) that straddles the River Nadder.

Wilton Weaving Works

Wilton is also famous for its carpets, an industry founded by the 8th Earl of Pembroke using French Huguenot refugee weavers. The original ★ **Wilton Weaving Works** (King Street,; tel: 01722 744919; open Monday to Saturday 9am–5pm and Sunday 11am–5pm) is open to the public and you can take factory tours to see how Wilton carpets are produced today .

While in Wilton, don't miss the ★ **parish church**. Built in 1841–5, it is a brilliant example of neo-Romanesque architecture, incorporating a magpie's hoard of ancient Roman columns, Italian mosaics, Flemish Renaissance woodwork, and German and Dutch stained glass.

Route 6

Winchester

High Street – Great Hall – Regimental museums – Cathedral – College – Meadow Walks – Hospital of St Cross – Wolvesey Castle – Riverside Walk – Bridge Street and The Broadway.

Winchester shared the honours of joint capital of England with London until the 12th century, and it was from this city that royal visitors would set out on their hunting expeditions to the New Forest. The city's attractions are many and varied and you should devote a full day to exploration.

Winchester's car parks are well signposted on the approach roads to the city centre. Most are on the redeveloped south side of the city, only one or two blocks from the pedestrianised **High Street**, where the geographical centre of the city is marked by the 15th-century ★ **Butter Cross**, greatly restored by George Gilbert Scott in 1865 and featuring a statue of King Alfred, under whose patronage the city first blossomed as a medieval centre of learning in the 9th century.

High Street and Butter Cross

From this point the city's main street heads uphill to **Winchester Castle ⑧**, now the site of Winchester's Law Courts, scene of infamous trials, such as that of Rosemary West and of the unfortunate heroine of Hardy's *Tess of the*

ROUTE 6
WINCHESTER
0   200m
0   200yds

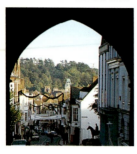

A distant 'Horse and Rider'

D'Urbervilles. Alongside the Elizabeth Frink sculpture of a *Horse and Rider* (1975), a steep flight of steps leads up to the ★★ **Great Hall** ❾, which is all that remains above ground of the castle, first built by William the Conqueror in 1067 (open: daily 10am–5pm, but closes 4pm at weekends November to February). This bare 13th-century hall is of great historic importance, for it was here that Henry III held court and assembled his informal parliaments, though the administrative centre of the kingdom was already shifting decisively towards London.

Henry's son, Edward I, the last king to live in the castle, was probably responsible for the famous **Round Table** that hangs on the Great Hall's end wall. Tree-ring dating points to construction between 1250 and 1280, though it was the youthful Henry VIII who had the table painted in 1520 with the Tudor Rose in the centre and portraits of the 24 Knights of the Round Table around the edge (King Arthur being a portrait of Henry). Henry's intention was not to convince anyone that the table had been used by the legendary knights, but rather to symbolise the antiquity of his own lineage.

38

Beneath the table is a fine bronze of an imperious Queen Victoria, the work of Sir Arthur Gilbert, presented to Hampshire in 1887 to mark the queen's Golden Jubilee.

A small doorway in the north wall of the hall leads to **Queen Eleanor's Garden**, named after Eleanor of Provence, wife of Henry III, and designed in the style of a medieval bower. The garden leads to the Peninsula Barracks, site of a palace designed by Sir Christopher Wren for Charles II but never completed. The army took over the site and the present barrack buildings are now being converted into luxury townhouses.

Five army museums ❿ remain on the site, and a visit here provides the opportunity to explore a relatively un-

The Great Hall's Round Table

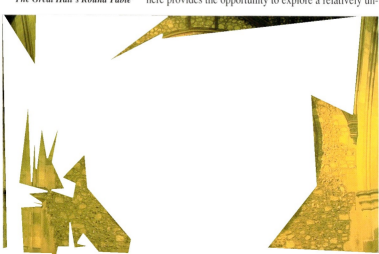

known corner of Winchester, set high enough up to afford fine views down onto the cathedral. The army museums (tel: 01962 864176 for all five) are well presented, and more absorbing than you would, perhaps, imagine.

The **★ Royal Hussars Museum** Tuesday to Friday 10am–4pm, weekends noon–4pm) contains uniforms, dioramas and memorabilia from wars in Africa, India, and the Crimea, including the Charge of the Light Brigade. The **★ Light Infantry Museum** (Tuesday to Saturday 10am–5pm, Sunday noon–4pm) contains a large graffiti-covered chunk of the Berlin wall, and covers such recent conflicts as Cyprus, Northern Ireland and Bosnia.

The **★ Royal Hampshire Regiment Museum** (Monday to Friday 10am–4pm, weekends noon–4pm) has displays on the two world wars, and the **★ Royal Green Jackets Museum** (Monday to Saturday 10am–5pm, Sunday noon–4pm) contains a diorama of the Battle of Waterloo, with sound and light show. If you only see one museum, that of the **★ Brigade of Gurkhas** is perhaps the most interesting (Tuesday to Saturday 10am–5pm) because of its lively tableaux illustrating the history of the regiment and the lives of its Nepalese servicemen.

Leaving the Peninsula Barracks site by the main gate, turn right to pass through the medieval **Westgate**, one of the two surviving defended gateways in Winchester's city walls. A small **★ museum ⑪** on the first floor displays armour, weights and measures, prisoners' graffiti and a 16th-century painted wooden ceiling (tel: 01962 869864; open same hours as City Museum – *see below*).

The **★★ City Museum ⑫**, also small but crammed with finds from the last 30 years of excavation in Winchester, is reached by returning down the High Street to the Butter Cross and turning right through the narrow alleyway alongside to reach The Square (Monday to Saturday 10am–5pm, Sunday 2–5pm, or to 4pm in October to March; tel: 01962 863064). The museum provides hands-on activities for children (make your own mosaic, identify various animal bones) while grown-ups take in the model of the Saxon minster, precursor to the cathedral, carved Romanesque capitals, Saxon hogsback tombs and a fine 9th-century purse reliquary. Upstairs are old shops and a luxurious Edwardian bathroom suite rescued from Westgate House, while the top floor is devoted to Roman finds, including intact Samian ware vessels, Rhenish glass vessels, and beakers made in the New Forest potteries established around AD250.

Across the green lawn from the City Museum is the entrance to the **★★★ Cathedral ⑬** (daily 7.15am–6.30pm). Before setting out to explore this rewarding building, you may want to visit the information desk (tel 01962 853137) to pre-book tickets for one of the tours. Tours of the cathe-

39

West Gate

City Museum

dral depart on the hour, and there are two tours daily of the crypt. On Wednesdays and Saturdays, you can also join tours of the roof and tower.

Every corner of this majestic building – the longest medieval church in Europe at 556ft (169.5m) – is rich in historical and architectural detail. Like so many great cathedrals, this one was no sooner completed and dedicated in 1093 than work began on remodelling parts and adding others, so that all styles and periods of medieval ecclesiastical architecture are represented here. The **nave**, with its soaring stone lierne vault, belongs to the 14th-century Perpendicular era. A popular spot in the **north aisle** is the **grave of Jane Austen** [A] (her simple stone slab details her sweet temperament, but makes no mention of her great skills as a novelist), which is found close to the 12th-century black Tournai marble font [B], richly carved with scenes from the Life of St Nicholas.

The **north transept**, boldly Romanesque in style, is one of the oldest surviving parts of the church, dating from the first building campaign of 1079–98. On the right, the **Holy Sepulchre Chapel** [C] contains 12th-century frescoes of Christ's entombment, while the **Epiphany Chapel** [D] has Burne-Jones windows. The crypt is entered from this transept: Antony Gormley's bronze statue in the centre of the crypt looks especially effective when reflected in the shallow flood waters that fill the crypt for much of the year.

From the steps that lead up into the choir and retrochoir, the whole of the east end of the cathedral is floored in medieval tiles. The **choir** has England's oldest cathedral stalls, dating from 1305–10. The undersides of the seats are carved with irreverent and humorous scenes. The stone screen around the chancel is topped by mortuary chests containing the bones of Saxon kings, including Cnut, Egbert and Ethelwulf.

Back in the ambulatory, the Renaissance **chantry chapel of Bishop Gardiner** [E] is more imposing, though the stone carving of the cadaver below the chapel warns of the end that

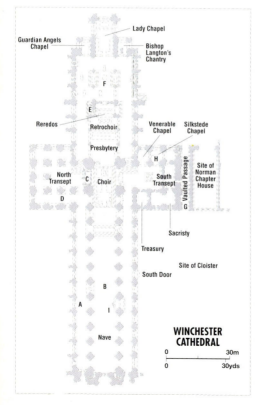

Lady Chapel
Guardian Angels Chapel
Bishop Langton's Chantry
F
E
Reredos
Retrochoir
Venerable Chapel
Silkstede Chapel
Presbytery
H
North Transept
C Choir
South Transept
Vaulted Passage
Site of Norman Chapter House
D
G
Sacristy
Treasury
Site of Cloister
South Door
B
A
I
Nave

WINCHESTER CATHEDRAL

0   30m
0   30yds

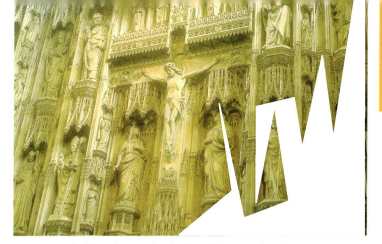

comes to us all. Other chantry chapels, like miniature cathedrals covered in elaborate tracery, fill the **retrochoir**, though St Swithun [F], the 9th-century Bishop of Winchester, whose feast day (15 July) is said to tell us whether or not it will be a rainy summer, only gets a modern metal canopy over the spot where his shrine stood until its destruction in 1538.

The **Lady Chapel**, the easternmost part of the church, has paintings on the Life of the Virgin and 16th-century stalls. To the south of the chapel entrance [G] is a bronze sculpture commemorating William Walker who worked in his diving suit to underpin the subsiding east end of the cathedral six hours a day for six years from 1900.

Returning down the south side of the church, the transept contains entrance to the **Cathedral Library**, where the precious 12th-century Winchester Bible is on display. Here too, in the southernmost chapel, is the grave of Izaak Walton (1593–1683) [H], author of *The Compleat Angler*, and a stained-glass window of 1914 depicting Walton seated beside the River Itchen in the watermeadows just outside Winchester. If this scene tempts you to follow Walton's example, leave the cathedral by the west door, first paying your respects to William Wykeham [I] (1324–1404), founder of Winchester College, whose magnificent tomb is on the south side of the nave.

Turn left as you leave the cathedral, and left again down the little alley that leads into the ★★**close**. Bear right, following signs for Winchester College, passing the fine medieval buildings that remain from the **Priory of St Swithun**, mostly now used as residences for the bishop and clergy. Keep following the signs until you exit from the close alongside the Pilgrim's School, with its 14th-century timber-framed buildings, passing through the wisteria clad gatehouse into St Swithun Street.

*Reredos
and cloisters*

Window on the close

Here, on the left, is **Kingsgate**, the second of the city's surviving medieval town gates, with the little church of ★ **St Swithun** above. Pass through the arch, and turn left into college street, where Jane Austen spent the last weeks of her life (at No 8) ⑮ writing her posthumously published novel, *Persuasion*. The buildings to the right belong to ★★ **Winchester College** ⑯, one of England's premier public schools, founded by William Wykeham in 1382. Its chapel is rich enough to rival the cathedral (open daily by guided tour in March to September at 11am (not Sunday), 1pm and 3.15pm, tel: 01962 868778).

At the end of College Street you have the option of heading right down College Walk, and right again past the green-roofed college concert hall to find the riverside path that crosses the Itchen watermeadows to ★★ **St Cross Hospital**, just under a mile south of the city. The walk is well worth while just to see the magnificent Norman chapel attached to the **almshouses**, founded in 1136 and Britain's oldest surviving charitable institution. The hospital still hands out the Wayfarer's Dole, consisting of a piece of bread and a small cup of beer, to travellers who ask for it at the porter's lodge, following a custom established in the 12th century. The almshouses have 13 pensioner residents, and visitors can see the medieval kitchen, the chapel, the hall and the Master's garden (open April to October 9.30am–12.30pm and 2–5pm, November to March 10.30am–12.30pm and 2–3.30pm, tel: 01962 851375.

42

Follow the riverside path

As you return across the meadows, with St Catherine's hill, topped by an Iron-Age hillfort to your right, reflect on how many works of literature have been inspired by this spot. Trollope was inspired to use the St Cross Hospital as the setting for his first Barchester novel, *The Warden*, and Keats wrote his best-loved ode, *To Autumn*, whilst walking these meadows on a misty September day in 1819.

Back at College Walk, you can visit the ruins of ★ **Wolvesey Castle** ⑰ (English Heritage; tel: 01962 854766; open 1 April to 31 October, 10am–16pm, or dusk if earlier) to see the imposing and extensive remains of the Bishop of Winchester's former residence. From the castle, a delightful walk passes between the chalk, flint and brick walls of the castle and the River Itchen, leading to St Swithun's bridge and **City Mill** ⑱, the latter built in 1744 and now belonging to the National Trust, which intends to restore the waterwheel to full working order.

King Alfred

Turning right here will take you up to the well-named **Broadway**, with its bronze statue (1901) of King Alfred the Great, and the Abbey Gardens ⑲, a pretty public park, on the left. Beside the park is **Abbey House**, the official residence of the mayor, and finally the **Guildhall**, a fanciful 19th-century French-style Gothic building which houses the tourist information centre.

Route 7

The Test Valley

Stockbridge – Danebury Hill – Houghton Lodge Gardens – Mottisfont Abbey – Romsey – Broadlands – Hillier's Arboretum

In its upper reaches, the River Test is one of England's most delightful rivers, a sparkling chalk stream that continually splits and rejoins as it meanders southwards through the chalkland landscape to the north of the New Forest, flowing through public gardens and the grounds of stately homes, though ending its days rather sadly at Totton, amidst the drear landscape of motorway flyovers and industrial estates on Southampton's western edge. You can walk the valley of the Test, following the Test Way long-distance footpath, a total of 46 miles (74km), but few of us have the time, so here is a tour that covers the main sites in a day.

Contemplating the Test

★ **Stockbridge** is the Test Valley's unofficial capital, an attractive town with a wide main street, lined by handsome Regency buildings. The Test runs to the west of the town where the banks are usually lined by anglers fishing for brown trout. Stockbridge is ringed by low hills that nearly all have Iron-Age encampments on their summit, none more impressive than that on Danebury Hill, 3 miles (5km) northwest of the town.

Stockbridge

43

The ★ **Danebury Ring Iron Age Hill Fort** is both an archaeological site of international importance, and a huge outdoor adventure playground, with massive ramparts to scale and ancient beech trees to serve as hiding places during a mock attack. There is also a signposted walk around the 13-acre (5-hectare) site, making the most of the elevated position and magnificent views.

The archaeological importance of the site relates to excavations carried out by Barry Cunliffe in the 1970s and '80s during which he sought to establish what these hillforts, which are found throughout Europe, were actually used for. Did Iron-Age people live in them, or were they just used as a stronghold in the event of an attack?

Danebury

Professor Cunliffe has concluded that the site was probably a tribal gathering place from as early as the beginning of the 1st millennium, and may have served the combined functions of marketplace, religious site and venue for outdoor festivals. Any large tribal gathering would be vulnerable to attack from empire-building neighbours, who might take the opportunity to wipe out a whole clan in one fell swoop, hence the elaborate system of ditches and ramparts, which were built as symbols of power and status

Houghton Lodge

The Whistler Room

Mottisfont suntrap

as well as for practical defence. Here there is evidence of an attack that took place around 100BC, after which the site fell out of use.

Pleasanter thoughts are evoked by the pastoral beauty of the Test Valley as you head south along the minor road to ★ **Houghton Lodge** (March to September Monday, Tuesday and Friday 2–5pm and weekends 10am–5pm, tel: 01264 810177). Here you can wander through attractive gardens surrounding a fine example of an 19th-century cottage ornée, built in 1801 (possibly designed by the architect Nash) with neo-Gothic windows and tall chimneys. Despite being called a cottage, this lodge is built on quite a large scale and is a typical product of the romantic picturesque movement that was popular amongst the idle rich at the beginning of the 19th century.

Continuing along the minor road through Houghton village, we reach another aristocratic domain at **Mottisfont**, 4 miles (6km) further south. ★★ **Mottisfont Abbey** (National Trust; tel: 01794 340757; open 1 April to 31 October, Saturday to Wednesday noon–6pm or dusk if earlier, open daily noon–8.30pm in June) is packed to the gills in June when visitors come by the coachload for the famous collection of old-fashioned scented roses. At other times of year the house and gardens still have much to offer and are far more tranquil.

Mottisfont, set amidst lush watermeadows beside the Test, was chosen in 1201 as the site for a priory of the Austin Canons, which thrived until the Black Death carried away most of the monks and left the order impoverished. The Dissolution finished off the monastic institution and the estate was acquired by the Lord Chancellor, William Lord Sandys (he paid a high price, giving the two villages of Chelsea and Paddington to the Crown in return for these rolling Hampshire acres).

Sandys built the Tudor mansion at the heart of today's estate, incorporating parts of the monastic buildings, and the house underwent further alterations in the 18th and 19th centuries. The most intriguing room in the house is the **Whistler Room**, named after the artist who painted its *trompe-l'oeil* decorations during 1938–9. The stucco work, pilasters and trophy panels are a triumph of illusionistic art; best of all is the alcove draped with a stole, black glove and wedding ring, carelessly piled with books as if Mrs Russell, who commissioned the work, had been seated there until just a moment ago.

The **gardens**, though, are the real triumph of Mottisfont. The formal parterres immediately around the house were laid out in 1936–7 under the supervision of Geoffrey Jellicoe. The **Walled Garden**, some distance from the house, was planted in 1972–3 as a showcase for the National Trust's collection of historic roses, ranging from the original red and white roses of the houses of Lancaster and York, to popular hybrids developed in the 19th century. Quite apart from the scents, the colours and the eye-pleasing forms of these roses, the garden is a stimulating object lesson in how to grow roses – not in boring beds where no other plants are allowed to thrive, but up and through trees, over arches and pergolas, and underplanted with all sorts of perennial and annual plants.

Garden-loving visitors to Mottisfont will surely want to take in the world-famous Hillier Gardens and Arboretum *(see below)* but it is worth stopping first in **Romsey**, 4 miles (6km) downstream, for the splendid Norman ★★ **abbey church** that is the burial place of Earl Mountbatten of Burma (1900–79). The first nunnery here was founded in AD907 and Saxon remains from that era are visible through the trap door in the north transept. There is also a remarkable Saxon crucifix, carved in stone and set into the west wall of the south transept. The present church, of 1150–70, exhibits all the features that typify English Romanesque architecture: blind arcading, zig-zag arches and corbels carved with beasts and demons.

Abbey church and interior

Before he was murdered by an IRA bomb while sailing in County Sligo, Earl Mountbatten lived at ★★★ **Broadlands**, the stately home that lies just south of the town (open 1 July to 31 August daily, noon–4pm, tel: 01794 517888;). An exhibition here focuses on the role of Earl Mountbatten as supreme commander of the Allied forces in southeast Asia from 1943–45, and as the last Viceroy of India, appointed to oversee India's transition to independence from British rule. The house is also remembered as the place where Prince Charles and Princess Diana began their honeymoon.

Three miles east of Romsey, between the villages of Ampfield and Braishfield, is the world-renowned ★★★ **Hillier Gardens and Arboretum** (open daily, except for Christmas and New Year bank holidays, 10.30am–6pm or dusk, if earlier, tel: 01794 368787). Extending to 166 acres (66 hectares), these lovely gardens were founded in 1953 by Sir Harold Hillier, the nurseryman, as a home for his collection of some 42,000 different varieties of trees and shrub. Highpoints of the year are late spring and early summer, when the rhododendrons and azaleas are in full bloom, and the autumn when the trees are cloaked in richly coloured leaves.

Hillier Arboretum

The gardens are not just for tree lovers: in the area around Jermyns House, Hillier's former home, there are extensive ponds, bog, swamp, scree and peat gardens, all supporting specialist communities of plants.

Route 8

Southampton and the Isle of Wight

Waterfront and city walls, Tudor House Museum, Maritime Museum, Museum of Archaeology, Tudor Merchant's House, Civic Centre and Art Gallery, Eling Tide Mill

Southampton's city walls
Titanic memorial

Southampton is the port from which the *Mayflower* set sail for America in 1620 and the *Titanic* set out on her ill-fated voyage in 1912. At this port countless colonial administrators, deportees, emigrants and luxury cruise passengers have embarked on ships that have carried them half-way round the world. Even with the decline of sea transport, Southampton remains a busy passenger and container port. Flattened by German bombers during World War II, the city is today largely the result of post-war planning, but Southampton makes the most of its heritage, with a number of museums clustered around what remains of the medieval walls.

To the Isle of Wight

Southampton also attracts visitors en route to the **Isle of Wight**. Red Funnel Ferries (tel: 01703 330333) operate services at hourly intervals throughout the day, and you can choose between the speedy hydrofoil service (crossing time 22 minutes), which goes to West Cowes, or the slower conventional ferry (55 minutes) to East Cowes. East and West Cowes stand on opposite banks of the Medina Estuary, and there is no linking bridge, though there is a regular chain ferry linking the two parts of the town.

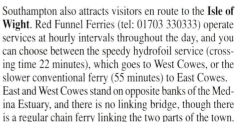

East Cowes is best if you want to visit ★★★ **Osborne House** (English Heritage; tel: 01983 200022; open April to October daily, 10am–5pm), which is 1 mile (1.6 km) to the east, and therefore within walking distance, of the ferry terminal. The house was Queen Victoria's private retreat from royal duties, and it was designed by her husband, Prince Albert, assisted by Thomas Cubitt, in 1845. Victoria died here in 1901, and the house remains largely as it was at the time of her death, having been given to the nation shortly after the event by Edward VII.

The Italianate style of the house is in marked contrast to the neo-Gothic that was fashionable in the mid-19th century, and it fits well with the formal splendour of the gardens, across which Victoria liked to watch ships steaming out of Southampton to all corners of her vast Empire. The house is richly furnished, and is far from being the 'dear, modest, unpretentious Osborne' of Victoria's own description. The royal children even had their own house in the grounds – the Swiss Cottage, where they learned such useful accomplishments as gardening, carpentry,

The Swiss Cottage

cooking and sewing under their father's watchful eye.

Osborne House offers enough to keep visitors happy for a good part of the day, but if you have time to spare, consider heading for Newport, the island capital, and Carisbrooke Castle, a mile (2km) southwest of the town (to do this by public transport, take the No 4 bus from Osborne to East Cowes, the No 5 bus from East Cowes to Newport, then the No 7 to Carisbrooke Castle – there are frequent services on all these routes). **Newport**'s attractions include a handsome waterfront lined with 19th-century merchants' houses and warehouses, one of which is now the ★ **Quay Arts Centre**, housing craft workshops and art galleries. The **church** contains a fine effigy in marble of the sleeping Princess Elizabeth, daughter of Charles I, who died at Carisbrooke Castle of pneumonia in 1650. Queen Victoria paid for the monument in 1856, along with a memorial to Prince Albert, both by the 19th-century Italian sculptor Marochetti.

★★ **Carisbrooke Castle** (English Heritage; tel: 01983 522107; open daily 10am–6pm, but closes at 4pm in November to March) sits at the geographical heart of the Isle of Wight and was fortified from the 8th century. The 12th-century keep survives, but most of the surviving buildings date from the 16th century when England was threatened with invasion by Spain. Charles I was also held a prisoner at Carisbrooke in 1647 before being taken, via Hurst Castle, to London for trial and execution. There are exhibits relating to his imprisonment, but the star attraction is the 18th-century donkey treadmill (with live donkeys) which was used for drawing water up from the castle's 49m- (161ft-) deep well.

Back in Southampton, the place to head for is the ★★ **Tudor House Museum** ㉑ (Bugle Street; tel: 01703

Carisbrooke Castle

635904; open Tuesday to Friday 10am–noon and 1–5pm, Saturday to 4pm and Sunday 2–5pm). This magnificent merchant's house, built for the Dawtrey family in 1495, will convince you that there was nothing inferior about Tudor timber-framed houses, for this is a spacious and elegant building full of material relating to domestic life in the city through the ages, including a Georgian wing, a Victorian kitchen and a display of Victorian toys in the attics (look out for Mr Punch, and the voluminous bathing costumes).

Turning right from the museum, in Bugle Street, take the next right to reach **Westgate**, one of the surviving gates in the city walls. Follow the walls round to the left, passing the Mayflower Monument, and the onion-domed entrance to the **Royal Pier**, which opened in 1833. Cross Bugle Street to the ★★ **Maritime Museum 22** (Town Quay; tel: 01703 635904; open Tuesday to Friday 10am–1pm and 2–5pm, Saturday to 4pm and Sunday 2–5pm), housed in the Wool House, built in the late 14th century by the monks of Beaulieu Abbey as a warehouse for their wool exports. The magnificent building, with its fine oak and chestnut trussed roof, evokes the days when Southampton was the epitome of a modern port, from where the Queen Mary and other cruise liners departed for such exotic destinations as Brazil and the West Indies. Here you can see scale models of the port, and of the Queen Mary herself, posters advertising luxurious holidays, ships' engines, with completely inappropriate names like 'Venus', and an extensive display charting the ill-fated history of the *Titanic*.

Turning left out of this museum, it is a short stroll to the ★★ **Museum of Archaeology 23**, located two blocks east in the God's House Tower, part of the city's medieval defences (Winkle Street; tel: 01703 635904; open Tuesday to

Maritime Museum

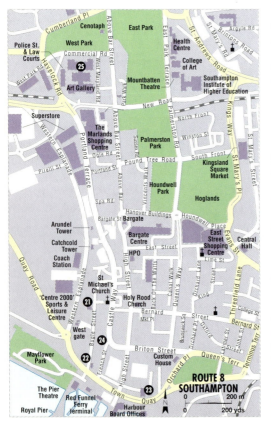

Friday 10am–noon and 1–5pm, Saturday to 4pm and Sunday 2–5pm). Though small, the museum packs in a surprising amount of information on Clausentium and Hamwic, the Roman and Saxon predecessors, respectively, of modern Southampton. Particularly interesting is the account of the Saxon town, refounded in AD690 among the ruins of the Roman city, and rapidly developing into a thriving port, exporting grain, wool, cloth and slaves, and importing fine pottery, wine, spices, honey, silk, fine cloth, building timber and stone.

Stretching north from the museum is a footpath that follows the most complete surviving stretch of the town walls, with information boards explaining the purpose of the interval towers. Where the lane ends at Briton Street, turn left and walk two blocks to the ★ **Medieval Merchant's House** **24** (English Heritage; 58 French Street; tel: 01703 221503; open April to October daily, 10am–6pm). Built in the 13th century as a shop and home for the wine merchant John Fortin, the timber framed house has been furnished as it might have looked when newly built. The gaudily coloured cabinets, chests, wall hangings and furnishings will come as a shock to those who think of medieval houses in terms of sombre earth colours, but the restorers claim that this is the real thing, and no pastiche.

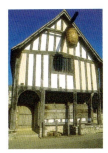

Medieval Merchant's House

Crossing one block east, and walking up the long **High Street**, will take you to the northernmost gate in the medieval city walls, the majestic ★ **Bargate**, richly decorated with battlements, arches and a statue of George III. North of here begins the modern pedestrianised shopping precinct. If you continue to the top, and turn left in Centre Road, you will come to Southampton's wonderfully adventurous ★★ **Civic Centre** **25**, designed in the style of an Inca palace in 1932–9 by E. B. Webber. Housed in the north wing is the **City Art Gallery** (Tuesday, Wednesday and Friday, 10am–5pm, Thursday to 8pm, Saturday to 4pm and Sunday 2–5pm). The collection is unusually rich in early 20th-century art, including works by Duncan Grant, Stanley Spencer, Matthew Smith and Gaudier-Brzeska, and it has numerous works by living artists, such as Allen Jones and Peter Blake. Many works are shown by rotation, but a room is given over to a permanent display of Burne-Jones's dramatic series of paintings illustrating the legend of Perseus.

49

Bargate

An old tune

If you are heading back to the New Forest from Southampton, there is one last sight on the outskirts of Southampton to consider: the 18th-century ★ **Eling Tide Mill**, just off the A35 at Totton (Wednesday to Sunday, 10am–4pm, tel: 01703 869575) is the only working mill of its type, built across an inlet on the estuary of the Test to harness the power of the tide for milling wholemeal flour.

Route 9

Gosport, Fareham and Portchester

Titchfield Abbey – Fort Brockhurst – Gosport – Fort Nelson – Portchester Castle

There is no escaping from the military theme of this day, but only born-again pacifists will find it difficult to enjoy the submarine tour and Fort Nelson armoury museum that are the focal point of this tour.

Approaching from the west, Gosport is signposted from junction 9 of the M27. This leads on to the A27 through ★ **Titchfield**, where the **Abbey** is worth a brief halt (English Heritage; tel: 01703 226235; open daily 10am–6pm in April to October, 10am–4pm or dusk rest of year). 'Abbey' is perhaps a misnomer, for the site consists principally of the magnificent Tudor gatehouse built by the Earl of Southampton when he acquired the monastery at the Dissolution. Titchfield itself is a fine village with much good Georgian brick architecture, and the ★ **church** contains an outstanding double monument to the first and second earls of Southampton, dated 1594.

Continuing into **Gosport**, you will not be able to miss **Fort Brockhurst**, so massive are its brick-faced ramparts topped by green turf and surrounded by a moat (English Heritage; tel: 01962 868944; open daily 10am–1pm and 2–6pm or dusk if earlier). This massive structure was built during the 1850s as part of a ring of coastal defences intended to protect the Gosport peninsula and the naval dockyards at Portsmouth from invasion by France. Fort Brockhurst is one of the last in a line of military castles that stem back to the medieval period, even to Roman times, differing not greatly in layout and function from Portchester Castle (*see below*), built in the 4th century AD. A novel feature here is the use of earth and grass to roof the perimeter buildings, both as a disguise and for aesthetic reasons, to minimise the visual impact of the vast fortress on the landscape.

To reach ★★ **Submarine World**, continue into the heart of Gosport, following signs that take you over a causeway to the very tip of the Gosport peninsula. The museum (daily 10am–5.30pm, but to 4.30pm from November to March, tel: 01705 529217) starts with an audio-visual explaining the basics – how subs use their ballast tanks to dive below the surface of the seas and rise back again – before you are led off on a guided tour of the real thing. Sadly *HMS Alliance* is now suspended in dry dock, beside Gosport harbour, so visitors do not get to go below the waves, but you can look through the periscope, and the guides, all retired submarine servicemen, play record-

Fort Brockhurst

Early submarine

Scene in Gosport

ings that give you an idea of the sound of the massive engines turning on and the ship preparing to dive. You are left with an impression of life on board being extremely dangerous, cramped and smelly, with poor food, lack of privacy and hard beds all thrown in for good measure.

The museum opposite *HMS Alliance* continues the theme of submarine warfare, tracing the early history of man-powered torpedoes through to the modern nuclear-powered submarines capable of staying below water for months on end. This museum also features a periscope and, if it is not being monopolised by small boys, you can look through it for a view of Portsmouth harbour.

★ **Gosport Museum** is in the town centre's pedestrianised precinct (Walpole Road; open Tuesday to Saturday 10am–5pm, Sunday 1–5pm. This is a typical local history museum with one difference: it has an excellent geology display which uses a mock-up of a time-machine to take children on an audio-visual journey through geological time, back to the very first stirrings of life on earth. The formation of fossils is explained before viewers are let loose to explore cases full of dinosaur bones, sharks' teeth and fascinating minerals, all found on the fossil-rich shores around Gosport.

Leaving Gosport on the A32, head for Fareham and then follow the brown road signs for Fort Nelson. You will find yourself climbing to a ridge located high above Portsmouth harbour with outstanding views. ★★ **Fort Nelson** is part of the same Victorian ring of defences as Fort Brockhurst, a massive brick and turf structure from which artillery would have been able to shower mortars down onto any would-be attacker in the harbour. Today it houses the **Royal Armouries Museum of Artillery** and, by virtue of the live demonstrations that take place throughout the day, calls itself, with justice, Britain's loudest museum (April

Submarine World Marina

Artillery at the ready, Fort Nelson

Portchester Castle

Reliving the glories of the past

to October daily, 10.30am–5pm). Here you can see a section of the Iraqi supergun, along with examples of artillery through the ages. More exciting is the warren of underground ammunition tunnels, which are fun to explore, and the reconstructions of 19th-century kitchens and mess rooms, illustrating the hardships of barracks life.

From one of England's most recent fortifications, we descend to one of the oldest. ★★ **Portchester Castle** sits on the foreshore between Fareham and Portsmouth, its walls lapped by the waters of Portchester Harbour (English Heritage; tel: 01705 378291; open daily 10am–6pm, but to 4pm from November to March). The walls surrounding the castle represent the most complete remains of any Roman fortification in Europe.

Portchester was one of a chain of fortresses built in the 3rd century AD along the eastern and southern coast of England, from the Wash to the Solent. Collectively they are known as Saxon Shore Forts because they were built in response to raids by Saxon pirates from northern Germany and the Low Countries. The fortress continued to be occupied almost without interruption throughout the post-Roman and medieval period, being used as a walled settlement, a castle, and a royal palace, then as a military hospital in the 17th century, and finally as a prison until well into the 19th century. Only then did it become a picturesque ruin.

If you have a head for heights, scale the Norman keep on the landward side of the fort for fine views, looking out as you go for graffiti scratched into the walls by French prisoners-of-war. It is also well worth taking a close look at the church exterior, even if the church itself is locked. The west front, with its zigzag moulding, is a fine example of mid-12th century Romanesque work, and the nave walls contain plenty of reused Roman tile and masonry.

Route 10

Portsmouth and Southsea

Charles Dickens's birthplace – Portsmouth Historic Dockyard – Old Portsmouth – Southsea

If you are interested in ships, the sea and all things nautical, Portsmouth is the place for you. It is the perfect place to take children with piratical leanings – here they can find out what it was like to live and fight on a ship. Portsmouth is rewarding, but you need to plan in advance what you want to see. There are enough sights to keep you busy for two full days – one spent at the Historic Dockyards, another spent touring the Old City – while a third could be spent taking in the Isle of Wight.

Dickens's birthplace

Portsmouth is a large and confusing city, the result of post-war reconstruction which gave pride of place to the car, though the main sights are easily found because they are signposted on all the approach roads. Without following the signs, you would never find the ★ **Charles Dickens Birthplace Museum**, located in the northern suburbs, at 393 Commercial Road (open daily April to October, 10am–5.30pm, tel: 01705 827261).

This cobbled backwater, where Dickens was born in February 1812, escaped the World War II bombing that flattened so much of the city centre. Dickens's father, John, was a clerk in the Navy Pay Office and he moved here in 1809 with his young bride, Elizabeth. Great efforts have been made to recreate the appearance of the house as it was when Dickens's parents were tenants.

As you continue your journey south, following the brown 'Historic Ships' signs, Portsmouth's character as a naval garrison town becomes

ROUTE 10
PORTSMOUTH

0   400 m
0   400 yds

Spit Sand

Henry VIII

Mary Rose plates

HMS Victory

increasingly apparent. Despite bombing, a good number of fine 18th and early 19th-century buildings have survived in the area around the harbour, and the best of these can be seen as an incidental part of a visit to see the historic ships, *Mary Rose*, *HMS Victory* and *HMS Warrior*. An inclusive ticket allows you to visit all three, and to explore a number of museums all dotted around the 300-acre ★★★ **Historic Dockyard** (open daily, except Christmas and Boxing Day, 10am–4.30, with extended opening hours in summer). On arrival you will be given a timed ticket for the guided tour of *HMS Victory*; otherwise you are free to wander on your own.

If you like to do things in chronological order, then start with the **Mary Rose Exhibition ㉖**, in the first building on the right. A video explains the history of Henry VIII's flagship and is at pains to correct a common misconception, that the warship sank on her maiden voyage; in fact, she was built at Portsmouth in 1509–11 and saw 34 years of service before she sank 1 mile (2km) from Portsmouth Harbour on that fateful day in 1545. The video explains why she sank – she was overloaded, turned too fast, with her gun ports open, took in water and went to the bottom in minutes, taking with her most of the crew and all their possessions. It is these possessions, and what they tell us about Tudor life and warfare, that make the rest of the exhibition so rewarding. Case after case is filled with intriguing exhibits – violins and trumpets, arrows and longbows, food remains and the skeletons of rats, books, quill pens, surgical equipment and carpenter's tools, hats, boots and jerkins.

With your appetite whetted, head for the **Mary Rose Ship Hall ㉗**, alongside *HMS Victory*, and see what remains of the ship itself – not a soggy bit of broken timber, but a very substantial and impressive part of the hull and deck, continuously sprayed with a solution of polyethylene glycol as part of a conservation programme that will not be complete until well into the 21st century. Visitors to the hall are given a radio wand that picks up a fascinating commentary on the history of the ship and its construction.

Live commentators take tours round **HMS Victory ㉘**, repeating a fund of anecdotes about the unpleasant nature of life on board ship – maggoty biscuits, foul water and frequent floggings with a cat-o'-nine-tails being the lot of the average 18th-century sailor, if you believe what you are told. Apart from the pathos of Nelson's death on board this ship, the other striking feature is the similarity of *HMS Victory* to the *Mary Rose* – the conviction will grow, as you tour the warship *HMS Warrior*, later in the day, and as you visit the Submarine Museum at Gosport (*see page 50*) that fighting ships simply got bigger with time, but their basic structure and layout have scarcely changed in more than 500 years.

From beside the dry dock where *Victory* is moored, there are good views over the oldest surviving parts of the Portsmouth Dockyard, including the **Great Basin** which Peter the Great visited in 1698, and an array of workshops, foundries and storehouses built in the 18th and early 19th centuries, some to the designs of Isambard Kingdom Brunel. To get an idea of what went on in these buildings, visit the **Dockyard Apprentice Exhibition**, which uses waxwork tableaux to explain the main trades involved in ship construction. If your children catch sight of the indoor adventure playground in the same building, you may have difficulty dragging them away.

Perhaps you can bribe them with the promise of a **harbour tour**: this is not included in the admission price to the Historic Dockyard, but is good value, with boats departing at regular intervals from the mooring beside **HMS Warrior** **㉙**. The latter ship is a huge and impressive ironclad warship, the first of her kind, launched in 1860. You are allowed to scramble up and down the ship's ladders and wander at will, though there are guides as well who will explain aspects of life on board and give demonstrations of cannon firing.

Of the other two main museums on the site, the **Victory Gallery** contains a fascinating and detailed account of the Battle of Trafalgar, with a panorama and sound effects, while the **Royal Naval Museum** gives an exhaustive – and exhausting – account of British naval history, from the 18th century to the present day.

Old Portsmouth lies well to the south of the Dockyard, past Portsmouth Harbour railway station and the adjacent passenger ferry that takes commuters over the har-

Nelson commemorated

55

Royal Naval Museum

bour to Gosport, and past the Isle of Wight ferry terminal. It is a dreary 15-minute walk, so consider driving and parking on Grand Parade, which is well situated for exploring Portsmouth city centre and the adjacent seaside resort of Southsea.

Portsmouth's High Street contains the unfinished ★Cathedral ㉚ founded in 1927, but incorporating the elegant Early English chancel of the former parish church, dedicated to St Thomas of Canterbury and founded in 1180, just 10 years after his martyrdom. The cathedral naturally contains numerous monuments to naval personnel, and a memorial carved by Nicholas Stone to Charles Villiers, Duke of Buckingham and advisor to Charles I, who was murdered by an aggrieved soldier in the High Street in 1628.

Old Portsmouth
Portsmouth's Cathedral

If you continue up the High Street, you will pass **Buckingham House ㉛**, where the murder took place. Turning right at the top of the High Street, in Museum Road, will bring you to the ★★**City Museum and Records Office ㉜** (open daily, 10am–5.30pm, tel: 01705 827261) which contains some enjoyably nostalgic reconstructions of a 1930s kitchen, a 1950s living room and of Verrechias ice-cream parlour, where teenagers used to date in the 1960s. The audio-visual programme on the **Story of Portsmouth** leads on to exhibits covering prehistoric and Saxon finds, and there is an art gallery displaying crafts and paintings by contemporary artists.

Return south via Thomas's Street, which runs parallel to the High Street and is lined by Georgian houses, then turn left in Lombard Street and right to where the High Street ends by the ★**Square Tower ㉝**. This carries a gilded bust of Charles I and a chain-link sculpture commemorating the sailing of the first convict ship bound for Australia in 1787. An arch by the tower leads to the sea wall, which you can climb for harbour views. The seawall walk leads north to the ★Round Tower ㉞ of 1415, built to defend the harbour entrance.

Royal Garrison Church

In the other direction, via Grand Parade, you reach the ★**Royal Garrison Church ㉟**, where Charles II married his Portuguese bride, Catherine of Braganza, in 1662 (English Heritage; tel: 01962 86894; open April to September, Monday to Friday 11am–4pm). Originally this was part of a medieval hospital, later serving as an armoury and residence before conversion to a church. The nave remains a shell after fire bombing in 1941, but the chancel survives in its medieval form.

From the church, steps lead up to the **Long Curtain ㊱**, a 17th-century fortification that leads through Pembroke Gardens and Southsea Common to **Clarence Esplanade** in Southsea, a walk of about 1 mile (1.6km). Southsea has the air of a seaside resort, but with plenty of rainy-day activities. The ★★**Sea Life Centre**, on Clarence Esplanade (tel: 01705 734461; open daily 10am–5pm and later in summer) lets you feed stingrays, learn how to handle live crabs, watch newly hatched baby sharks in the nursery and view their grown-up counterparts, along with myriad other sea creatures, from the safety of a walk-through tunnel. **South Parade Pier** has a large funfair, and the ★★**Natural History Museum** (Cumberland House, East Parade; tel: 01705 827261; open daily 10am–5.30pm, but to 4.30pm in November to March) has live butterflies flitting around, an aquarium containing typical river fish, walk-through badger setts and fox holes, and a full-size replica of an Iguanadon.

The fun of the fair, Southsea
At the D-Day Museum

More for adults, perhaps, than children is the ★★**D-Day Museum** (daily 10am–5.30pm, but to 5pm in November to March) on Clarence Esplanade, home to the 272-ft (83-m) Overland Embroidery telling the story of the Normandy landings, backed up by an excellent film show and waxwork tableaux of life at home and at war in the 1940s.

Right next door is ★★**Southsea Castle** (open April to October daily, 10am–5.30pm, rest of year weekends only, 10am–4.30pm). Built by Henry VIII in 1545, the history of the castle is explored by means of a time tunnel and audio-visual show. The D-Day theme is picked up again by the ★★**Royal Marines Museum**, at the Eastney end of the Esplanade (open 10am–4.30pm daily, September to May, 9.30am–5pm in summer). The D-Day Encounter recreates, through films, artifacts and a mock-up of a field camp, events leading up to the Allied invasion of Normandy, and there are recreations of jungle and Arctic warfare, commando training and the Falklands campaign.

Portsmouth has two **Isle of Wight** ferry services, both going to the eastern side of the island (enquiries and reservations, tel: 01705 827744). The ferry to Fishbourne takes around 35 minutes, but for those in a hurry, the Ryde hovercraft completes the journey in under 15 minutes (passenger only).

To the Isle of Wight

Fishbourne doesn't have a huge amount to offer, so, unless you are planning to take the car and tour the island, **Ryde** is the better bet for a day trip to the island. There are plenty of Regency and Victorian buildings to remind us that Ryde became a popular resort during the early 19th century, and the Royal Victoria Arcade offers good browsing amongst antique shops and boutiques. To the typical seaside attractions of a seafront Promenade, mini-golf and trampolining, a canoeing and boating lake, dance halls and a fine sandy beach, there is a half-mile long pier offering fine views out to the ships passing up and down the Solent.

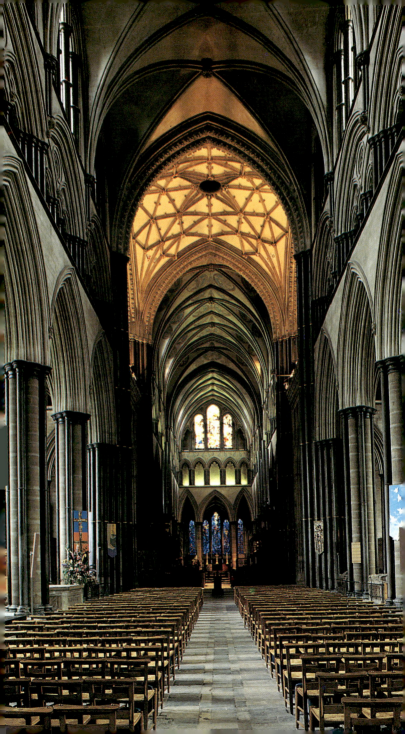

Architecture

Buildings of architectural elegance and stature can only be built where there is a ready supply of good building stone. In the case of the New Forest, with its underlying geology of gravel, sand, clay and chalk, building stone was such a scarce resource that it was reserved only for defensive structures – castles and town walls – or for prestigious buildings constructed for the glorification of God – abbeys, priories and cathedrals.

So scarce was stone that good masonry was recycled: Beaulieu Abbey was largely demolished so that Henry VIII could build a string of coastal castles, Old Sarum cathedral's stone was reused to build the houses of Salisbury's cathedral close, while the town walls of Winchester and the masonry cladding Wolvesey Castle were suitably redeployed.

Timber was, by contrast, relatively plentiful, but there was competition for this resource from the region's shipbuilding industry – around 60 acres (23 hectares) of woodland provided enough mature timber to build just one of the 67 naval and merchant ships constructed at Bucklers Hard, and this was only one of the New Forest's shipyards. Great cathedrals such as Winchester also took their toll: when Bishop Walkelin began work on the first cathedral in 1070, William the Conqueror rashly promised him all the timber he could cart in four days from the royal forest of Hempage Wood, near Alresford. At the end of four days, it is said, only one tree was left standing.

Houses in and around the New Forest were therefore built of poorer timber, known as scantlings, or of mud bricks made of a mixture of dried clay, straw and dung, known as cob. Inevitably, buildings of this type have not survived in great quantity, despite the impression given in postcard views of thatched timber cottages. Instead, most were replaced with brick buildings from the mid-18th-century when brick began to be produced in quantity and distributed via England's extensive canal network.

Driving around the New Forest you will see many early brick farm buildings, and brick is the predominant material used in the handsome townhouses of Lymington, Christchurch and Winchester. Of course, if you were wealthy enough, you could always import timber, and the magnificent Tudor House Museum in Southampton shows that timber need not be second best when it comes to creating spacious and luxurious living accommodation.

Church architecture

By contrast with the relative plainness of the domestic architecture, the New Forest area has some fine examples of church architecture from every period. The con-

Old Sarum

Thatch and timber cottage
A closer look at thatch

Portchester Castle
Romsey Abbey

Winchester Cathedral detail

quering Normans introduced to England the bold, and sometimes outlandish forms of Romanesque architecture, well represented at Christchurch Priory, Romsey Abbey, Winchester Cathedral and the Hospital of St Cross. Characteristic of this style is the round, or hemispherical arch, so simple that it could have been drawn with a compass, fat circular pillars without any kind of moulding, and cushion capitals, often, by contrast with the pillars, elaborately carved with stylised foliage or miniature biblical scenes. Exaggerated zigzag carving, sometimes also known as dogstooth, is used to decorate doorways and arches, as at Portchester Castle and Romsey Abbey, and arcading – sometimes blank, sometimes elegantly formed from pairs of arches separated by a central shaft, provides geometric patterning at Winchester and Christchurch.

As English masons, taught by their French counterparts, began to grow in confidence, they developed their own distinctively English versions of the international Gothic style. Early English architecture succeeded Romanesque in the early 13th century, and one of the finest examples is the retrochoir at Winchester, which in turn had a considerable influence on Salisbury Cathedral, England's most complete and harmonious example of the style. Early English is characterised by tall pointed lancet windows, grouped in threes or fives, often with the central window taller than those either side, separated by clusters of thin shafts instead of one single mullion or column.

There is a purity and single-mindedness about Early English which leaves some people cold while others regard it as the zenith of English medieval architecture. To those who subscribe to the latter view, the Decorated style that evolved from Early English in the late 13th century is a degenerate and overly elaborate architectural form, but looking at the flowery geometric patterning of the west window at St Cross or the tracery of the cloisters at Salisbury Cathedral, it is hard to be so censorious.

The last stage in English Gothic is the Perpendicular style, so-called because the ornate and flowing tracery characteristic of the Decorated period, based on arcs of circles and with no straight lines anywhere to be seen, gives way to style firmly rooted in strong vertical lines emphasising the height of buildings and windows; Winchester Cathedral's west front and nave being perfect exemplars of the style.

At ceiling level, Perpendicular architecture breaks free of rectilinear restraint, and both the nave at Winchester and the chantry chapels of the retrochoir are covered in the flamboyant vaulting that became a trade mark of English cathedral masons for a century or so, from the mid-14th century until the iconoclasm of the Tudor period and the end of the great era of English church architecture.

The Arts

Holidaymakers of the past expected to be entertained when they went to the seaside, and, as a legacy of the end-of-pier shows and brass band concerts, Bournemouth has a thriving arts and entertainment's scene. Depending on your taste you can watch rock bands, popular TV comedians or musicals at the Pier Theatre, at the seaward end of Bournemouth Pier, the Pavilion Theatre, Westover Road, or the Bournemouth International Centre, Exeter Road, or listen to the world-renowned Bournemouth Symphony Orchestra (BSO) at the Winter Gardens Theatre, Exeter Road (all four theatres share the same box office number for information and bookings; tel: 01202 297297).

Member of the Bournemouth Symphony Orchestra

When the BSO is not playing at the Winter Gardens, it is probably alternating with rock and folk bands or plays and musicals at one of the other major arts venues around the region, including the Southampton Guildhall (tel: 01703 632601), the Turner Sims Concert Hall in Southampton (tel: 01703 595151) or the Portsmouth Guildhall (tel: 01705 824355).

61

Bournemouth also offers plenty of free entertainment. Every Friday at 10pm during the July to September school holidays, the pier is used as the launchpad for a fireworks extravaganza. During the same period, anyone strolling in the Lower Gardens can listen to bands playing most mornings and afternoons in the Pine Walk Bandstand.

Festivals occur throughout the season, kicking off with the Southampton Film Festival in early March (tel: 01703 635335), moving on to two folk festivals at Gosport over Easter (tel: 01705 484242) and in Winchester at the end of April (tel: 01962 870081). The region's biggest event is the Bournemouth International Festival in May, a two-week celebration of all the arts (tel: 01202 297327) followed shortly afterwards by the Salisbury Festival (tel: 01722 323888). Events throughout the season also take place in the grounds of Beaulieu (tel: 01590 612123) and Broadlands (tel: 01794 517888), ranging from classic car rallies to open-air promenade concerts with fireworks.

Heavy Horse Parade, Portsmouth

For something more traditional, there are occasional Heavy Horse parades in Portsmouth and pony sales which take place five times a year, in April, August, September, October and November (for precise dates, which vary from year to year, call the New Forest Visitor Information Centre; tel: 01703 282269). Up to 500 ponies can be sold at each auction sale which begins around 8.30am at the market next to Beaulieu Road railway station, midway between Lyndhurst and Beaulieu. Apart from the opportunity to savour the festive atmosphere and gain an insight into the working life of the Forest, there are stalls selling all sorts of crafts and horse-related products.

Food and Drink

The New Forest has no culinary specialities that it can truly call its own, though, with the sea so close, fish features on many a restaurant menu, and mushroom lovers should look for dishes using locally picked penny buns (ceps) and chanterelles. French influence on the region's cooking is very strong, and many of the top restaurants use buyers based in France to send fresh produce over daily on the cross-Channel ferries.

Restaurants

£££ = over £60 for two; **££** = £40–60 for two; **£** = under £40 for two (including house wine).

Bournemouth, Christchurch and New Milton

£££Marryat Restaurant, Chewton Glen, Christchurch Road, New Milton, near Bournemouth, tel: 01425 275341. Chewton Glen has established a reputation as one of Britain's top hotels (*see page 79*) and its restaurant (Michelin Star Award) is as good as you would expect from such an establishment. Neither, in luxury hotel terms, is it especially expensive. Good value set-price menus allow you to sample what the restaurant does best: top-quality ingredients, with the emphasis on local fish, cooked simply and without unnecessary ostentation.

Fine cuisine at Marryat

££Ocean Palace, 8 Priory Road, Bournemouth, tel: 01202 559127. Near the seafront, behind the Bournemouth International Conference Centre, this smart Chinese restaurant features an extensive menu of Cantonese, Beijing and Shanghai-style food, with some excellent seafood and vegetarian dishes.

££Mr Pang's, 234 Holdenhurst Road, Bournemouth, tel: 01202 553748. Chinese cooking comes into its own when the ingredients are as fresh as possible, and Mr Pang makes the most of the locally caught fish – try eating it steamed with ginger and spring onions.

££Sea View Restaurant, Haven Hotel, Banks Road, Sandbanks, tel: 01202 708796. With such a banal name you would expect stodgy English fare, but the Sea View (so named because there are fine views from the terrace to Studland Bay) turns out such tasty French-inspired dishes as angler fish with ratatouille and pigeon salad. For those who like traditional English food, Sunday lunch is a serve-yourself buffet with roasts.

You cut and I'll choose

££Splinters, 12 Church Street, Christchurch, tel: 01202 483454. Expect some unusual and inventive dishes on the menu of this bistro-style restaurant, alongside desserts that attract members of the Chocolate Society to hold regular meetings here and an excellent choice of British and Irish cheeses.

Toby Hill at Provence

£Fisherman's Haunt, Winkton, near Christchurch, tel: 01202 484071. After scrambling up Hengistbury Head, come and relax in the pub's gardens by the River Avon and stoke up on sausages and chicken nuggets (children are welcomed), cold meats and fish from the carvery, or the daily specials chalked up on the blackboard.

£Chez Fred, 10 Seamoor Road, Westbourne, Bournemouth, tel: 01202 761023. One of England's top fish-and-chip restaurants, with queues for the takeaway section trailing around the block at the height of summer. The walls are covered with photographs of the celebrities who have popped in for cod and chips after performances at the Pier or Pavilion theatres; popular favourites are the Catch of the Day, and the Feast for a Fiver (cod, chips, mushy peas, roll, butter and a glass of beer or wine).

Lymington and Beaulieu

£££Provence, Gordleton Mill Hotel, Silver Street, Hordle, tel: 01590 682219. Toby Hill, who trained under Raymond Blanc, presides as chef over this restaurant with rooms (*see page 79* for hotel details) set in a 17th-century water mill, offering dishes in the grand French manner with an outlook over ponds, weirs, gardens and mill machinery.

££ –£££Rocher's, 69–71 High Street, Milford on Sea, near Lyminton, tel: 01590 642340. The set-price menus at this French bistro-style restaurant change daily according to what is best in the market, though there is always a good balance of fish and meat dishes to choose from and a lot of effort goes into the deservedly popular desserts.

££Le Poussin, The Courtyard, Brockley Road, Brockenhurst, near Lymington, tel 01590 623063. This tiny courtyard restaurant (25 seats within, three tables outside if the weather is fine enough) really makes the best of local food: wild mushrooms, Itchen trout, and locally reared wild pork (a wild boar/domestic pig hybrid) all feature regularly on the menu, though the all-time favourites, which customers return for again and again, are the trio of meats (beef, lamb and venison), followed by the chocolate terrine.

£Chequers, Ridgeway Lane, Lymington, tel: 01590 673415. Full of weekend yachting fanatics who come to sustain themselves on filled French sticks at the bar, or more substantial meals in the pub restaurant. Mussels, fresh grilled fish, a vegetarian and a pasta dish always feature on the daily changing menu.

£Red Lion, Boldre, near Lymington, tel: 01590 573177. Traditional pub food, including basket meals, but with some non-traditional extras, such as an excellent vegetable casserole for non meat eaters, and partridge in white wine for the carnivores.

£Montagu Arms, Palace Lane, Beaulieu, tel: 01590 612324. As a pleasant alternative to the institutional 'school-meals' served up in the café at the Beaulieu Palace and Motor Museum, head for this rambling hotel just outside the palace gates and enjoy either a full meal in the dining room, or good snacks in the bar. Outdoor tables, children welcomed.

£The Master Builder's House, Bucklers Hard, tel: 01590 616253. This is a charming 18th-century house with lots of olde world nautical atmosphere (*see page 78 for hotel details*) serving good pub food, with a fine garden sweeping down to the boat-filled marinas of Southampton Water.

The Master Builder's House

Portsmouth and Southsea

££Bistro Montparnasse, 103 Palmerston Road, Southsea, tel: 01705 816754. This French bistro, designed to appeal to Continental visitors heading to or from the ferry ports, offers stylish dishes as part of a very good value daily set menu, all accompanied by home-baked bread served with olive oil.

£Still & West, Bath Square, Portsmouth, tel: 01705 821567. Children are welcomed at this friendly pub in old Portsmouth, with its model ships and extensive harbour views from the first-floor restaurant. Fish and chips are served at the bar, as well as excellent ploughman's lunches (with a choice of some 12 or more different cheeses). Upstairs, fresh fish is the staple.

Rockbourne (near Fordingbridge)

£Rose and Thistle, tel: 01725 518236. After visiting Rockbourne Roman Villa, come to one of Hampshire's prettiest villages for top-quality bar food in this thatched 17th-century inn. Lunchtime stalwarts include homemade soups, ploughman's and sausages, filled pancakes, casseroles and pies. Evening meals include steaks and fresh fish.

Romsey

£££Old Manor House, 21 Palmerston Road, Romsey, tel: 01794 517353. Despite the English name and setting, this is a seriously Italian establishment where you can feast on fresh pasta, game, wild mushrooms and truffles (all found locally), cured meats (smoked in the manor's giant fireplace), and locally caught trout and lobster, plus a few necessary imports from Italy (genuine Parma ham, for example).

Old Manor House

Winchester

££Old Chesil Rectory, 1 Chesil Street, tel: 01962 851555. Claiming to be one of the oldest buildings in Winchester, the Old Chesil Rectory is suitably low ceilinged and, for those who imbibe too much during their meal, the sloping floors can prove a challenge. The French-influenced food is flavoursome and filling: try symphony of fish or port-marinaded pigeon.

££Wykeham Arms, 75 Kingsgate Street, tel: 01962 853834. Deceptively disguised as an ordinary city pub, albeit a very civilised one, with a golden patina and warming log fires, the restaurant here is so widely renowned that bookings are essential. The style is English with French overtones (ie the roast Hampshire Down lamb comes with Provençal vegetables, the cod with onion confit, and so on). A welcome touch is the Alternative Beverage List, offering a whole range of non-alcoholic drinks, including such nursery favourites as Horlicks and Bovril. If the weather is fine enough, opt for one of the tables in the walled garden.

£–££Hotel du Vin & Bistro, 14 Southgate Street, tel: 01962 841414. The name of this restaurant with rooms set in a fine 18th-century house signals that wine is as important as the food here, as you might expect from an establishment which is run by the former sommelier (in partnership with the former managing director of Chewton Glen: *see page 79*). What is pleasantly surprising, given this impressive background, is to find that the restaurant is very good value for money, offering efficient but friendly service, simple wooden tables, and unpretentious bistro food, notably chargrilled steaks of pork, beef or tuna. With wines from all over the world to choose from, the range extends from inexpensive *vin du pays* to many of the finest clarets.

Pub-grub is an inexpensive option

Shopping

Day trippers from the Continent head for the English Channel ports to shop, so Southampton, Bournemouth and Poole are well supplied with all the usual British chain stores, from Marks & Spencer and the Body Shop to Virgin Records and branches of booksellers Waterstones. Shopaholic cravings of a more individual kind are satisfield in Salisbury and Winchester which have pedestrianised precincts lined with more offbeat boutiques and speciality shops. Winchester is of particular interest on account of its antique shops, and Salisbury has a number of fine antiquarian bookshops in the streets leading to the Close.

The list that follows singles out some of the more unusual shopping areas, markets and factory outlets in the New Forest area. In particular, it points you towards working mills and potters, where you can see for yourselves fine goods in the making.

New Forest gifts at the Witches' Coven, Burley

Whitchurch Silk Mill, 28 Winchester Street, Whitchurch (tel: 01256 892065). This working silk mill just north of Winchester, still uses machinery installed before World War I, driven by a water wheel of 1890. You can tour the mill to see the silks being woven, watch a video on the history of the building and visit an exhibition of historic costumes (mainly 18th- and 19th-century).

Gorgeously coloured furnishing and dress fabrics are available for sale, and if you are wealthy enough, like the international decorator clients who regularly come to buy from Whitchurch mill, you can have textiles woven to your own requirements. Alternatively, the mill sells a range of attractive and reasonably priced ties and scarves which make good gifts.

Poole Pottery, Poole Quay, Poole (tel: 01202 666200). The pottery at Poole, especially known for the collectable art nouveau and arts and crafts designs produced earlier this century, still produces cheerful and brightly patterned handmade and hand-painted pottery. Visit the museum, watch the video detailing the company's history and take a tour of the factory, perhaps even trying your hand at making your own pot, before browsing in the extensive shop alongside. The shop stocks a range of British crafts generally, not just Poole Pottery's own products – though it sells these as well, including a good selection of seconds at bargain prices.

Wilton Carpet Factory, King Street, Wilton (tel: 01722 744919). Just outside Salisbury, the Wilton Carpet factory offers another chance to combine a factory tour with a shopping expedition. The shop here sells both first-quality Wilton carpets and rugs at factory prices, and it sells

Gosport town centre

bargain-priced seconds. In addition, a clothing shop sells designer label men's women's and children's fashions and household linens.

Wimborne Market, Wimborne Minster (tel: 01202 841212). If you cannot resist browsing for bargains – and know the worth of what you are buying – this is the market for you. It is one of the most extensive markets in Southern England and well patronised by old-hands in the antiques and bric-a-brac trade. The market site is huge and attracts anything up to 500 stalls (half of them indoors, half out). The Friday market (7am–2.30pm) specialises in antiques, while the Saturday market (8am–1pm) is a flea and general market, and Sunday market (9am–4pm) is a bit pot luck, with absolutely everything on sale from cut-price pet foods and cheap jeans to good secondhand books and records.

King's Walk, Winchester (tel: 01962 862277). This antiques and craft centre, which has an extensive range of stalls, is just one of the reasons why British and foreign visitors flock to Winchester to shop for fine quality antique furniture, clocks, antiquarian books and other collectables. For a good selection of secondhand books and prints, head for Kingsgate Books in College Street, and for antiques generally wander around The Square and the Jewry Street area, where a good many items are sure to catch your eye.

Fisherton Mill, Fisherton Street, Salisbury (tel: 01722 415121). This design and contemporary craft emporium occupies several floors and includes an outdoor exhibition area where you can shop for fine art, jewellery, ceramics, furniture and textiles, children's toys and 'lifestyle' accessories.

Active Pursuits

The New Forest and the south coast are very popular as weekend destinations for every kind of outdoor activity. Here are the main centres and sources of information.

Cycling

Despite restrictions on which tracks cyclists may use in the New Forest, there is still plenty of opportunity to get well off the beaten track. As part of their hire package, the following bike hire shops offer a selection of routes:

AA Bike Hire, Fern Glen, Gosport Lane, Lyndhurst, (tel: 01703 283349)

Burley Bike Hire, Village Centre, Burley (tel: 01425 403584)

Cool Cats Leisure, Sandbanks Hotel, Sandbanks, Poole, (tel: 01202 701100)

New Forest Cycle Experience, The Island Shop (just opposite the railway station), Brookley Road, Brockenhurst, (tel: 01590 624204).

Testing the terrain

Diving

The Poole Dive Centre, Quaywest, West Quay Road, Poole (tel: 01202 677427)

Christchurch Sub-Aqua School (tel: 01202 485974)

Poole Marine Activities Base, Hamworthy Park, Lulworth Avenue, Poole (tel: 01202 673336).

69

Fishing

Hatchet Pond and Cadman's Pool, two of the larger ponds in the New Forest, are available for coarse fishing. They contain pike, roach, bream, tench, carp, perch, eels and rudd. No other ponds can be fished and trout fishing in the New Forest streams is also forbidden. The season is from 16 June to 14 March and anglers must hold a National Rivers Authority rod licence and buy a permit. Permits and further information can be obtained from the Forestry Commission Office, Queen's House, Lyndhurst (tel: 01703 283141). Post offices and fishing tackle shops in the region also sell permits.

The rivers Itchen, Meon, Dever, Avon and Test are all renowned amongst anglers for their trout. Advice on fishing grounds and permits can be obtained from:

Leominstead Trout Fishery, Emery Down, Lyndhurst (tel: 01703 282610)

The Rod Box, London Road, King's Worthy (tel: 01962 883600).

Sea fishing for mullet, bass, plaice and dabs is good all round the coast, and fishing is permitted from the lower stages of Bournemouth Pier. The following also offer deepwater fishing trips:

Fishing at Fordingbridge

Sea Fishing (Poole), Fisherman's Dock, The Quay, Poole (tel: 01202 679666)
Shark and Deep Water Angling, Keyhaven (tel: 01590 642366).

Golf

Dibden Golf Centre on the eastern edge of the New Forest is a parkland course with views over Southampton Water. The 18-hole course can be booked in advance, or you can just turn up for the 9-hole course on a 'pay and play' basis. PGA-approved instructors are available. Dibden Golf Centre, Main Road, Dibden, Southampton, SO4 5FB (tel: 01703 207508).

Teeing off

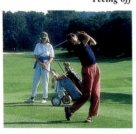

To the northeast of the New Forest, just off the A35 Winchester Road, the Southampton Municipal Golf Course offers two well-established 'pay and play' courses, an 18-hole par 69 course with a yardage of 6,313, and a 9-hole par 32 course over 2,385 yards. Services include tuition and equipment hire. For further details, tel: 01703 760546.

Bournemouth also has a municipal course, at Queen's Park (tel 01202 396198). The 6,505-yard 18-hole course has a par of 72.

Go-karting

Matchams Leisure Park, Hurn Road, off the A338 near Ringwood (tel: 01425 473305); go-karts, all-terrain jeeps, quadbikes.
Trackside Leisure, Unit 28, Solent Industrial Estate, Shamblehurst Lane, Hedgend, Southampton (tel: 01489 799294).

In pony country

Horse riding

With ponies such a strong theme in the New Forest, it's not surprising that opportunities for horse riding and pony trekking also abound. Riding stables in the New Forest area include:
Arniss Riding & Livery Stables, Godshill, Fordingbridge (tel: 01425 654114)
Burley Manor Riding Stables, Burley Manor Hotel, Burley, Ringwood (tel: 01425 403489)
Flanders Farm Riding Centre, Silver Street, Hordle, Lymington (tel: 01590 682207)
Forest Edge Stables, Oakdene Holiday Park, St Leonards, Ringwood (tel: 01202 897616).

Tennis

Bournemouth Tennis Centre, Central Gardens (tel: 01202 298570), has five artificial grass courts and three acrylic (the latter are indoors under an air dome from 1 October to the end of April). Equipment hire and professional tuition are available.

Sailing and watersports

Poole Bay and Christchurch Harbour offer safe, sheltered conditions for sailing enthusiasts, and most of the following organisations offer courses, tuition and hire.

Cool Cats Leisure, Sandbanks Hotel, Sandbanks, Poole (tel: 01202 701100); Hobie cat hire and sailing school.

Poole Yachts, 29 Branksea Avenue, Poole (tel: 01202 672155); skippered hire of 37-ft ketch.

Rockley Point School of Sailing, Rockley Sands, Hamworthy, Poole (tel: 01202 677272); dinghy and cruiser sailing tuition, windsurfing and boardsailing.

Sea Cruising Association, The Old Vicarage, 539 Ashley Road, Poole (tel: 01202 733996); yacht cruising and tuition.

Seascope Sailing School, 162 Lake Road, Hamworthy, Poole (tel: 01202 672442); dinghy sailing, weekend and weekly sailing tuition.

Bournemouth Surfing Centre, 127 Belle Vue Road, Southbourne (tel: 01202 433544); boogie boarding, surfing, windsurfing, boardsailing, equipment hire and tuition.

Ivy Lake Water Ski Club, Ivy Lane, Blashford, Ringwood (tel: 01425 471470); water skiing.

New Forest Water Park, off the A338, North Gorley, Near Ringwood (tel: 01425 656868); jet-skiing, water skiing.

Poole Harbour Boardsailing, 284 Sandbanks Road, Lilliput, Poole (tel: 01202 700503); windsurfing and boardsailing.

Sandbanks Boardsailing School, by the beach station, Shore Road, Sandbanks (tel: 01202 700503); windsurfing and boardsailing equipment hire and tuition.

Ski Rockley, Rockley Park Beach, Poole (tel: 01202 767848); water skiing, tuition, wetsuit and equipment hire.

Xtreme, 111 Commercial Road, Lower Parkstone, Poole (tel: 01202 741744); windsurfing and boardsailing.

An ideal coast for sailing

71

Messing about in boats

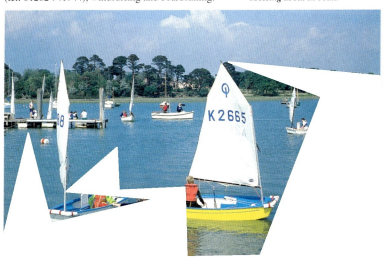

Getting There

Opposite: Portsmouth Harbour

By car

The New Forest is easily accessible by road from most parts of England, though the A34, M3 and M27 carry huge quantities of commuter traffic during the rush hours and of container lorries travelling northwards from Southampton docks. You should allow plenty of time to negotiate bottlenecks, in particular the approach roads to Ringwood and Newbury.

By coach

National Express operates in excess of 30 daily services from all parts of the UK to Bournemouth, Poole, Salisbury, Winchester, Southampton and Portsmouth.

For details you can phone the **TBC Hotline** (Train, Bus and Coach information for England, Scotland and Wales) on 0891 910910.

By rail

The New Forest is very well serviced by trains, with InterCity services to Southampton, and local trains from there to the heart of the New Forest (stations at Ashurst, Beaulieu Road, Brockenhurst, Lymington, Christchurch, Bournemouth and Poole amongst others). Some trains are linked directly to Isle of Wight and Continental ferry services at Southampton, Portsmouth, Lymington and Poole. Salisbury and Winchester are also on main Intercity lines. For information contact the Southampton enquiry office, tel: 01703 229393

By ferry

Southampton, Poole and Portsmouth are all linked to the continent by daily car and passenger ferries operating to Cherbourg, Caen, Le Havre and St Malo, in France, and Bilbao, in Spain. Contact your local travel agent for full details or telephone **Brittany Ferries**, Portsmouth (tel: 01705 827701), **P&O Ferries**, Portsmouth (tel: 01705 772244) and **Sealink Stena Line**, Southampton (tel: 01703 233973).

Sea connections are excellent

By air

The New Forest is served by two local airports. **Bournemouth International** (tel: 01202 593939) has regular scheduled flights to Paris, Brussels, Amsterdam, Dublin, Exeter, Humberside, Aberdeen and Manchester operated by **Euro Direct Airways** (tel: 0345 662222).

Southampton International (tel: 01703 620021) is located between Southampton and Eastleigh just north of junction 5 on the M27 and has regular flights to UK and Continental airports.

Getting Around

Public transport

With determination, you can get around the New Forest area using public transport, but you should expect to have to walk or use taxis to reach destinations that are not on bus routes. For comprehensive information on bus, rail and ferry services in the area, which will help you determine how feasible an option this is in the time you have available, contact the Passenger Transport officer at the address below and ask for free copies of the Public Transport Maps for Hampshire, and for the Portsmouth area (these maps are also available from tourist information centres in the region – *see page 75*).

Passenger Transport Officer,County Surveyor's Department, Hampshire County Council,The Castle, Winchester, Hampshire SO23 8UD. Tel: 01962 868944.

Taxis

Fleet Cars, Southampton, tel: 01703 466339
Lymington Taxis, tel: 01590 672842 and 673827
Salisbury Associated Taxis, tel: 01722 334477
Streamline Taxis, Portsmouth, tel: 01705 811111
Wessex Cars, Winchester, tel: 01962 877749

Car parks

There are – believe it or not – no less than 143 car parks dotted around the New Forest, many of them equipped with toilets, picnic areas and signboards with maps and suggested walks along waymarked walks. Finding somewhere to park is therefore not usually a problem, and the same is true of the big cities surrounding the Forest; all have large multi-storey car parks, well-signposted from every main approach road, but do not expect parking here to be cheap.

Yarmouth boat

Ferries to the Isle of Wight

All the following companies offer services at 30 or 60-minute intervals throughout the day.

Hovertrave: Southsea to Ryde (passenger). Tel: 01705 811000.

Wightlink: Portsmouth to Ryde (car and passenger); Portsmouth to Fishbourne (car and passenger); Lymington to Yarmouth (car and passenger). Tel: 01705 827744.

Red Funnel: Southampton to West Cowes (car and passenger). Southampton to East Cowes (car and passenger). Tel: 01703 330333.

White Horse: Southampton to Hythe (passenger). Tel: 01703 840722

Hurst Castle: Keyhaven to Yarmouth (passenger). Tel: 01425 610784.

Facts for the Visitor

Tourist information

Tourist information centres in the Forest region are run by knowledgeable and helpful staff.

Bournemouth, Westover Road, tel: 01202 451700

Bournemouth's TIC

Christchurch, 23 High Street, tel: 01202 471780
Fordingbridge, Salisbury Street, tel: 01425 654560
Gosport, Walpole Road, tel: 01705 522944
Havant, 1 Park Road South, tel: 01705 480024
Isle of Wight, Yarmouth Quay, tel: 01983 760015
Lymington, Waitrose Car Park, off High Street, tel: 01590 672422
Lyndhurst, New Forest Museum & Visitor Centre, High Street Car Park, tel: 01703 282269
Poole, The Quay, tel: 01202 673322
Portsmouth, The Hard (next to the entrance to the Historic Dockyard), tel: 01705 826722; also at 102 Commercial Road, tel: 01705 838382 and at the Continental Ferry Port, tel: 01705 838645

Ringwood, The Furlong, tel: 01425 470896
Romsey, 1 Latimer Street, tel: 01794 512987
Salisbury, Fish Row, tel: 01722 334956
Southampton, Civic Centre Road, tel: 01703 221106
Southampton Airport, tel: 01703 641261
Southsea, by the Sea Life Centre on Clarence Esplanade, tel: 01705 832464
Swanage, Shore Road, tel: 01929 422885
Winchester, The Guildhall, Broadway, tel: 01962 840500

Emergencies

In emergency dial 999 for all services.
AA Breakdown, tel: 0800 997766
RAC breakdown, tel: 0800 828282
Hayters Garage, Brockenhurst 24-hour breakdown service, tel: 01590 623122 (daytime), 0860 769924 (night)
Weather forecasts, tel: 0891 500403

Visitors to Swanage

Hospitals

The following have 24-hour emergency services:
Bournemouth, Castle Lane East, tel: 01202 303626
Lymington, Southampton Road, tel 01590 677011
Poole, Longfleet Road, tel: 01202 665511
Salisbury, Odstock Road, tel: 01722 336262
Southampton, Tremona Road, tel: 01703 777222
Winchester, St Paul's Hill, tel: 01962 863535

Police stations:

Bournemouth and Poole, tel: 01202 552099
Christchurch, tel: 01202 486333
Fordingbridge, tel: 01425 652222

Hythe, tel: 01703 845511
Lymington, tel: 01590 675411
Lyndhurst, tel: 01703 282813
Portsmouth, tel: 01705 321111
Salisbury, tel: 01722 411444
Southampton, tel: 01703 581111
Winchester, tel: 01962 868100

Spring blossoms

Forest rules

Every year hospitals deal with scores of people who have been bitten by Forest ponies, which are semi-wild and unpredictable in the way they behave. Equally, there are hundreds of collisions every year between drivers and ponies, deer, or other wild animals or grazing livestock. In order to prevent accidents, there are certain rules that the Forestry Commission and Verderers would like everyone to observe when in the Forest:

- Observe the 40 mph speed limit in force on all unfenced roads
- Do not stop beside the road to take pictures – only stop in designated car parks
- If you take pictures, stand between the animal and the road, so that you do not drive the animal into the road
- Never feed the animals
- Never come between a mare and her foal, a cow and her calf or a sow and her piglets
- Touching the animals can be dangerous, so keep a safe distance
- Keep dogs under control and do not let them near Forest animals
- Do not ride bikes, drive or park anywhere except where indicated
- Do not fly kites or model airplanes near animals
- Do not light fires
- If you are bitten by an adder, go straight to the nearest hospital

Accidents in the Forest involving wild animals (deer, foxes, badgers, etc) should be reported to the Forestry Commission, tel: 01703 283771.

If you see an animal (pony, cow, donkey, sheep or pig) injured or in distress in the Forest, try and identify its markings, brand or colourings, and locate the animal's position as closely as possible and inform the relevant Agister, or the police at Lyndhurst (tel: 01703 282813).

Agisters:
Northwest 0836 602163
Northeast 0836 203883
Southwest 0836 777525
Southeast 0836 500106.

The New Forest for Children

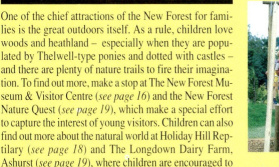
Having an adventure

One of the chief attractions of the New Forest for families is the great outdoors itself. As a rule, children love woods and heathland – especially when they are populated by Thelwell-type ponies and dotted with castles – and there are plenty of nature trails to fire their imagination. To find out more, make a stop at The New Forest Museum & Visitor Centre (*see page 16*) and the New Forest Nature Quest (*see page 19*), which make a special effort to capture the interest of young visitors. Children can also find out more about the natural world at Holiday Hill Reptilary (*see page 18*) and The Longdown Dairy Farm, Ashurst (*see page 19*), where children are encouraged to pet and feed the animals.

Within easy reach, at Bournemouth, but especially on the Isle of Purbeck – are some of the finest beaches in Great Britain. Bournemouth (*see page 27*) has a good range of wet weather possibilities, as does Southsea (*see page 56–7*), which has the Sea Life Centre, where one can feed stingrays or watch newly-hatched baby sharks, and South Parade Pier with its large funfair. Aspiring young naval officers will enjoy Portsmouth (*see pages 53–5*), where they can scramble up and down the ladders of *HMS Warrior* or find out about life on board *HMS Victory*, and the Submarine Museum at Gosport (*see page 50*).

The stately homes of the region also do their utmost to attract families. Wilton (*see page 36*) has one of the best adventure playgrounds in England, but for real theme-park thrills, visit Paultons Park, the New Forest's answer to Disneyland (*see page 18*).

Easy rider, Southsea funfair

Accommodation

Visitors to the Forest area are spoilt for choice when it comes to finding accommodation. Tourist Information Centres (*see page 75*) will book accommodation at all price levels, but to make your own arrangements, get hold of the well-illustrated brochure, *The New Forest – Where to Stay*, available from the New Forest Visitor Information Centre, High Street, Lyndhurst, Hampshire SO43 7NY (tel: 01703 282269; fax: 01703 284404), which gives information on every kind of accommodation, from deluxe hotels to cottages, campsites and caravan parks.

If you want to stay right in the heart of the New Forest, you should concentrate your attentions around Lyndhurst, Brockenhurst, Beaulieu and Lymington. The following list details characterful accommodation in this area. **£££** = more than £120 per night double; **££** = £90–120 a night double; **£** = £60–90 per night double.

Beaulieu
££Montagu Arms, Palace Lane, Beaulieu, Hampshire SO42 7ZL. Tel: 01590 612324. Fax: 01590 612188. Clad in Virginia creeper, this romantic-looking building feels far older than its actual date (it was built during the 1920s on the spot where the monks of Beaulieu originally had their guesthouse). The atmosphere of an Edwardian country house has been well recreated, with wood-panelled and book-lined public rooms. The best rooms are to the rear.
£The Master Builder's House, Bucklers Hard, near Beaulieu, Hampshire SO42 7XB. Tel: 01590 616253. Fax: 01590 616297. Converted from the 18th-century house of master shipwright Henry Adams, this hotel sits on the River Solent in the traffic-free village of Bucklers Hard, guaranteeing peaceful nights. Heavy beams, country-style furnishings and nautical memorabilia combine to make guests feel as if they are staying in a homely museum.

Country retreat

Brockenhurst
££Careys Manor, Brockenhurst, Hampshire SO42 7QH. Tel: 01590 623551. Fax: 01590 622799. This fine Arts and Crafts mansion of 1888 will appeal to the active: mountain bikes are available, and there is a pool, gym, sauna and children's playground. Rooms in the garden wing have balconies looking over the walled garden.
£Balmer Lawn Hotel, Lyndhurst Road, Brockenhurst, Hampshire SO42 72B. Tel: 01590 623116. Fax: 01590 623864. A former hunting lodge, this hotel sits in the midst of park-like grounds on the outskirts of Brockenhurst, with views over free-grazing ponies and cattle from the upper rooms. The extensive leisure facilities include swimming pools, tennis, squash, sauna and a gym.

£Whitley Ridge Hotel, Beaulieu Road, Brockenhurst, Hampshire SO42 7QL. Tel: 01590 622354. Fax: 01590 622856. A friendly small hotel in a secluded Georgian house set amidst parkland, with 13 rooms, views over woodland and fields. Cheerful log fires on cooler evenings.

Christchurch

£££Chewton Glen, Christchurch Road, New Milton, Hampshire BH25 6QS. Tel: 01425 275341. Fax: 01245 272310. Chewton Glen is one of England's best-known country house hotels, occupying an elegant 18th-century mansion. The swimming pool, familiar from features in so many style magazines, is modelled on the bathhouses of ancient Rome. There is a health club where you can work up an appetite before sampling the top-class cuisine in the restaurant (*see page 63*). Rooms come in all sorts of size and shape – choose between four-postered antiquity, chic modernism or country cottage style.

Chewton Glen

Lymington

££Gordleton Mill Hotel, Silver Street, Hordle, Lymington, Hampshire SO41 6DJ. Tel: 01590 682219. Fax: 01590 683073. Seven tastefully decorated bedrooms with en-suite whirlpool baths in converted 17th-century mill. Renowned for its Provence Restaurant.

££Passford House, Mount Pleasant Lane, Lymington, Hampshire SO41 8LS. Tel: 01590 682398. Fax: 01590 683494. The grand former home Lord Arthur Cecil is a white building with light airy rooms and a leisure complex with pools, solarium and sauna.

£Stanwell House, High Street, Lymington, Hampshire SO41 9AA. Tel: 01590 677123. Fax: 01590 677756. A smart hotel in an 18th-century building in the centre of Lymington. Guests can use the swimming, tennis and squash facilities at the nearby Elmers Court Country Club.

Lyndhurst

££Parkhill Hotel, Beaulieu Road, Lyndhurst, Hampshire SO43 7FZ. Tel: 01703 282944. Fax: 01703 283268. The best rooms in this rambling hotel have fine views over open parkland and lake (coarse fishing available to guests). There is a heated swimming pool and a conservatory restaurant specialising in modern British food.

£Lyndhurst Park Hotel, High Street, Lyndhurst, Hampshire SO43 7NL. Tel: 01703 283923. Fax: 01703 283019. Extended Georgian house on the edge of town, with views over the open Forest, tennis, sauna facilities and a pool.

£The Crown, High Street, Lyndhurst, Hampshire SO43 7NF. Tel: 01703 282922. Fax: 01703 282751. Antique-filled rooms in a characterful old house opposite Lyndhurst's hilltop church.

Crown Hotel, Lyndhurst

Index